John Fletcher

American Patriotism

Farther confronted with reason, scripture, and the constitution. Being

observations on the dangerous politics

John Fletcher

American Patriotism
*Farther confronted with reason, scripture, and the constitution. Being observations
on the dangerous politics*

ISBN/EAN: 9783337147242

Printed in Europe, USA, Canada, Australia, Japan

Cover: Foto ©Suzi / pixelio.de

More available books at **www.hansebooks.com**

AMERICAN PATRIOTISM

Farther confronted with

REASON, SCRIPTURE,

AND THE

CONSTITUTION:

BEING

OBSERVATIONS

ON THE

DANGEROUS POLITICS

Taught by the Rev. Mr. E V A N S, M. A.
And the Rev. Dr. P R I C E.

WITH

A SCRIPTURAL PLEA

For the REVOLTED COLONIES.

By J. FLETCHER, Vicar of MADELEY, Salop.

THE SECOND EDITION.

"Skill in *Politicks* contributeth not a little to the understanding
of divinity.—I learned more from Mr. *Lawson* than from any
Divine.—Especially his instigating me to the study of *Politicks*,
in which he much lamented the ignorance of divines, did prove
a singular benefit to me."

The Rev. Mr. R. Baxter's Life, p. 107, 108.

LONDON: Printed by R. HAWES,
And Sold at the Foundry in *Moorfields*; and at the
Rev. Mr. *Wesley's* Preaching-Houses, in
Town and Country. 1777.
[Price NINE-PENCE.]

PREFACE.

What diftinguifhes this Pamphlet from thofe which have been written on the fame fubject.—Nothing but SCRIPTURE and REASON can make the Colonies PROPERLY fubmit to Great Britain.

THE AUTHOR of thefe letters confiders the American controverfy chiefly in a *religious* light, which gives him an opportunity of making fome remarks, that have probably efcaped the attention of other writers on this fubject. The duty of paying taxes to the protective power, is fo ftrongly connected with chriftianity, that the Colonifts muft practically give up the fcriptures, or fubmit to the reafonable demands of the Britifh legiflature. It is to be wifhed, that we had made ufe of the Bible, in this controverfy. For, how much foever that venerable book is difregarded by fome of our great men, the bulk of the Americans, and our religious patriots in England, dare not defpife it. Mr. *Evans*, for one, fpeaking of the doctrine defended in thefe fheets, fays, " Should you indeed prove " it to be a SCRIPTURE-doctrine,. &c. I am " not afraid to *promife* you the moft abfolute " *fubmiffion* to it as a chriftian. The autho- " rity of SCRIPTURE I revere above every " other :" The contefted doctrine is here defended by fcripture againft Mr. Evans; and

A 2   if

if he stands to his " *promise,*" we may hope soon to see him give the Colonists an example of due " *submission.*"

When a great empire is divided against itself ;—when a powerful mother-country, and a number of strong Colonies, draw up all their forces to encounter each other in the field ;—when the two contending powers are subdivided into a warm majority and an heated minority, ready to begin a second intestine war ;—and when every individual is concerned as an actor, sufferer, or spectator, in the bloody tragedy which is acted ; it is natural for all lovers of their country to ask, How can the dreadful controversy be ended ? Is it by the dictates of scripture and reason, or by the force of Arms ?

If the author is not mistaken, Arms [tho' useful in their place] will never properly end the contest. Should we overpower the American Colonies, they will remain unconvinced. Far from being reconciled to their mother-country, they will still look upon her as an imperious step-mother, who adds tyranny to oppression, and murder to robbery. Nor will they submit to her any longer than the force, which has subdued them, shall continue to press and keep them down. And what shall we gain by this method, but perplexity, danger, and continual alarm? The condition of the Colonists will be as wretched as that of indignant prisoners, who are under a military guard : And our state will be as uncomfortable as that of a jailor, who watches over a numerous body of desperate captives, intent upon making their escape at the hazard of their lives. Under God, far more may then be

expected,

expected, in the issue, from scripture and reason than from arms. Beasts and savages can be conquered by fire and sword; but it is the glory of men and christians to be subdued by argument and scripture. Force may indeed bend the body, but Truth alone properly bends the mind. Whilst our armies prepare to engage the majority in America with the dreadful implements of war, it will not therefore be amiss to engage the ecclesiastical minority in England, with the harmless implements of controversy. On some occasions, one pen may do more execution than a battery of cannon: A page of well-applied scriptures may be of more extensive use than a field of battle: And drops of ink may have a greater effect than streams of blood. If a broad side can sink a man of war, and send a thousand men to the bottom; a good argument can do far more: For it can sink a prejudice, which fits out an hundred ships, and arms, it may be, fifty thousand men. How inferior then is the spear of Mars, to *the sword of the Spirit!* And how justly did Solomon say, *A wise man is strong*; especially if he is *mighty in the scriptures, which can make* us *wise to salvation!*

The author dares not flatter himself to have the knowledge of logick and divinity, which are requisite to do his subject the justice it deserves: but having for some years opposed *false orthodoxy*, he may have acquired some little skill to oppose *false patriotism:* And having defended *evangelical obedience to God,* against the indirect attacks of some ministers of the church of England; he humbly hopes, that he may step forth a second time, and defend also *constitutional obedience to* THE KING,

against

againſt the indirect attacks of ſome miniſters, who diſſent from the eſtabliſhed church. Thoſe whom he encounters in theſe ſheets, are the leading, eccleſiaſtical patriots of the two greateſt cities in the kingdom; Mr. *Evans* being the champion of the minority in *Briſtol,* as Dr. *Price* is in *London.*

The capital arguments of theſe two gentlemen are here brought to a triple teſt, againſt which they cannot decently object. And, if the author's execution keeps pace with his deſign, their politicks are proved to be contrary to *reaſon*, *ſcripture,* and the *conſtitution.* Should his proofs be found ſolid, and the publick vouchſafe to regard them ; the boiſterous patriotiſm, which has of late diſturbed our peace, will give place to ſober and genuine patriotiſm ; the political miſtake which produces our diviſions, will be plucked up by the roots ; the minds of our uneaſy fellow-ſubjects will be calmed ; our bloody conteſt for ſupremacy will give place to a ſweet debate between parental love, and filial duty : Parental love will overcome the Colonies with benign, lenient, and endearing offers of pardon and peace ; whilſt filial duty will diſarm the mother-country by kind, and grateful offers of manly ſubmiſſion.

C O N-

CONTENTS.

LETTER I.

The Arguments, by which Mr. Evans *tries to support his American politicks, are shewn to be contrary :* (I) *To sound reason:* (II) *To plain Scripture : And* (III) *To the British Constitution.*

LETTER II.

A view of Mr. Evans's *mistakes concerning :* (I) *The absoluteness of our property :*—(II) *The nature of slavery :*—(III) *The origin of Power :* —*And* (IV) *The proper cause of the war with* America.----*A note concerning the Anabaptists*

LETTER III.

Dr. Price's *politicks are shewn to be as irrational, unscriptural, and unconstitutional as those of Mr.* Evans.----*His principal arguments are retorted :*----*The foundation of his capital error is sapped :*----*The legislative freedom of the members of the house of commons is asserted, in opposition to the legislative pretensions of plebeian levellers :*----*The partiality and inconsistency of the* London-

A 4   *patriots*

patriots is pointed out :---On Dr. Price's *le-vlling principles there is an end of all fubjection both on earth and in heaven :---A conditional re-proof to Mr.* Evans *and Dr.* Price

L E T T E R IV.

Obfervations on Dr. Price's *awful arguments ta-ken from our immorality.---What great fhare our national prophanenefs had in the ruin of the king, and in the fubverfion of the church and ftate in the days of* Cromwell.---*It becomes us to obviate the dangerous argument, by which thoufands of rafh religionifts are feduced into wild patriotifm.*

L E T T E R V.

A fcriptural plea for the revolted Colonies ; with fome hints concerning a chriftian method of bring-ing about a lafting reconciliation between them and the mother-country.---An extract of a letter from Pennfylvania, defcriptive of American pa-triotifm :---And a remark upon a precipitate judgment of the Monthly Reviewers.

L E T-

AMERICAN PATRIOTISM, &c.

To the Rev. Mr. E V A N S,

LETTER I.

Rev. Sir.

THE Interests of Truth are often as much promoted, by the inconclusiveness of the arguments with which she is attacked, as by the force of the reasons with which she is defended. If my *Vindication* of the Calm Address has thrown some light upon the American controversy, your *Reply*, Sir, in the issue, may possibly throw much more. Supposing that plain Truth can be compared to a good steel; and keen error to a sharp flint; I venture to say, that the more any one strikes the steel with such a flint, the more will the fragments of the broken stone shew the superior solidity of the impugned metal; and the more easily will sparks be collected to light the bright candle of truth. The public will judge which arguments, yours or mine, will serve the cause of truth, by flying to pieces in the controversial collision.

Desirous to share the blessings, which our pacific Lord promises to the *meek* and the *peace-makers*; I shall, in these sheets, neither throw oil upon the flame of the American revolt, nor blow up the coals of indignation, which glow in the breasts of our insulted Governors. Whatever my performance and success may be, moderation and reconciling truth

A 5   are

are my aim: I can affure you, Sir, that my utmoft ambition is to draw the line between *unruly patriotifm* and *fervile fubjection*, in fuch a manner as to give you, and our readers, an equal deteftation of both thefe unconftitutional extremes.

After throwing away all your firft letter upon an ufelefs † queftion, and beginning the fecond with an idle ‡ report, you ftep into the tribunal of the Reviewers,

---

† This ufelefs queftion is, Whether Mr. Wefley had, or had not, forgotten the title of I know not what book, which he had recommended to fome of his friends, and which, thro' forgetfulnefs, he afferted that he had never feen ; till upon perufing the book, he difcovered and owned his miftake. Mr. Evans diverts the reader's mind from the true queftion, by fetting before him eight letters, which paffed between Mr. W. and others, about that infignificant particular. For my part I admit the public acknowledgment which Mr. W. has made of his forgetfulnefs rather than Mr. Evans's infinuation, that he is not " an honeft man ;" and I do it (1) Becaufe it is beft to be on the fafer fide, which is that of charity : (2) Becaufe it is highly improbable that a wife man, except in cafe of forgetfulnefs, would deny a fact, which a number of proper witneffes can prove, and are inclined to prove againft him : And (3) Becaufe experience conftrains me to fympathize with thofe, whofe memory is as treacherous as my own. On a Sunday evening, after preaching three times, reading prayers, and being all day in a croud, or hurrying from place to place, my mental powers are fo incapacitated to do their office, that, far from being able to recollect the title of a book, which I have feen fome months before ; I frequently cannot, after repeated endeavours, remember one of the texts, on which I have preached that very day. Now Mr. W. lives all the year round in the hurry and croud, in which I am on my bufy Sundays ; and he is between 70 and 80 years of age ; a time of life this, when even the men, who enjoy uninterrupted reft, find that their memory naturally fails. If Mr. Evans confiders this, he will not be furprized that his firft letter has not had its intended effect upon me.

‡ The idle report I mean is, that my Vindication " has received many additions and corrections from the pen of a celebrated nobleman." This is a miftake. I find indeed fome errors of the prefs, which injure the fenfe of my book ; but I do not difcover one addition in it, except that of *two* words ; and if Mr. Evans will be pleafed to infpect my manufcript, he will fee that the few little negative emendations in it, were made by Mr. Wefley's own pen.

viewers, and condemn my vindication before you
have refuted one of my arguments. As if you were
both judge and jury, without producing one true
witnefs, page 24, you authoritatively fay, " Inftead
" of argument, I meet with nothing but declama-
tion; inftead of precifion, artful colouring; inftead
" of proof, prefumption; inftead of confiftency,
" contradiction; inftead of reafoning, a ftring of
" fophiftries."

To fupport this precipitate fentence, you reprefent
me as faying things which I never faid. Thus
page 25, you write: " One while you tell us that
" our conftitution guards our properties, &c. againft
" the tyranny of unjuft, arbitrary, or cruel mo-
" narchs; then *you preach up with great folemnity,*
" &c. that their fubjects have no more right to *refift*,
" than children or fcholars have a right to take away
" paternal or magifterial authority." I defire, Sir,
you would inform me where I advance fuch a doctrine. Far from " *preaching it up with great folemnity,*" I abhor and deteft it. If a Nebuchadnezzar
commanded me to worfhip his golden image, I would
(God being my helper) *refift* him as refolutely as did
Shadrach. And fuppofe the king and parliament
were to lay a tax upon me, in order to raife money
for the purchafing of poifon, wherewith to deftroy
my fellow-fubjects, I would *refift* them, and abfolutely refufe to pay fuch a tax.

When you have made my doctrine *odious* by len-
ding me principles which I never advanced, or draw-
ing confequences which have not the leaft connexion
with my fentiments; you prejudice the public againft
my book, by infinuating, that I *contradict* myfelf,
where it is plain I do not. Thus you fay, p. 26,
" In one letter you tell us, *The Colonifts are on a
" level with* Britons *in general;* in another, that *They
" were never on a level with England.*" This laft
fentence I fpake of the *Colonies* as dependent legif-
latures, and not of the *Colonifts:* and both fentences
in their place are perfectly confiftent. For, altho"

not one of the COLONIES *was ever on a level with
England* (an INDEPENDENT KINGDOM) with refpect
to *fupreme* dominion ; yet all the COLONISTS *are on
a level with Britons in general,* with refpect to feveral
particulars enumerated juſt before, as appears by the
whole argument, which [Vind. p. 23] runs thus :
‘ The mother-country and the parliament-houfe are
‘ as open to them [the Coloniſts] as to any free-
‘ born Englifhman : they may purchafe free-holds,
‘ they may be made burgeſſes of corporate towns,
‘ they may be chofen members of the houfe of com-
‘ mons, and fome of them, if I miſtake not, fit al-
‘ ready there. *The COLONISTS are then on a level,*
‘ not only *with*’ [abfent] ‘ *Britons in general,* but
‘ with all our members of parliament who ARE A-
‘ BROAD.’ Had you, Sir, quoted my words in this
manner, your readers would have feen, that there is
fomething in my letters befides *contradiction* and *fo-
phiſtry* ; but it is far eafier to fhuffle the cards, than
to win the game.

Permit me, Sir, to produce another inſtance of
your polemical fkill : you fay, p. 24, “ Your rea-
“ foning upon the quotation I made from the very
“ learned Judge Blackſtone is equally conclufive,
“ &c. In a free ſtate (fays Judge Blackſtone) every
“ man who is fuppofed a *free agent,* ought to be in
“ fome meafure his own governor ; and therefore a
“ branch, at leaſt, of the legiſlative power fhould
“ refide in *the whole body of the people.* You reply,
“ —*Your fcheme drives at putting the legiſlative power*
“ *in every body’s hands.*” No, Sir, this is not my
“ reply, but only a juſt inference which I naturally
drew from my folid anfwer. My reply, Vind. p. 16,
runs thus : ‘ But who are *the whole body of the peo-
‘ ple ?* According to Judge Blackſtone, *every free
‘ agent.* Then the argument proves too much ; for
‘ are not *women* free-agents ? Yea, and *poor* as well
‘ as rich men.’ This, and this only I advanced as
a reply to Judge Blackſtone’s argument. I cannot
therefore help being furprized at your miſtake.—
                                                      You

You keep my real anſwer to your argument out of
ſight : You render me ridiculous by producing as
my anſwer, what is NOT my anſwer at all ; and, before you conclude, you make me amends for this
piece of patriotic liberty, by calling me " *one of the
moſt unmeaning and unfair controvertiſts."* The reader's patience would fail, were I minutely to de-
ſcribe the logical ſtratagems of this ſort, by which
you ſupport your cauſe, which I confeſs ſtands in
need of all manner of props.

However, in your ſecond letter, you come to THE
QUESTION, which is, Whether the Coloniſts, as
good men, good chriſtians, and good ſubjects, are
bound to pay moderate proportionable taxes, for the
benefit of the whole Britiſh empire ; when ſuch
taxes are legally laid upon them by the ſupreme
protective power, that is, by the three branches of
the Britiſh legiſlature.

In my *Vindication of the Calm Addreſs,* I have
produced the arguments which induce me to believe, that the doctrine of ſuch taxation is *rational
ſcriptural,* and *conſtitutional :* And in your *Reply* you
attempt to prove, that it is contrary to *reaſon, ſcripture,* and the *conſtitution.* Let us ſee how your attempt is carried on, and,

FIRST, how you diſprove the REASONABLENESS
of the taxation I contend for.

Page 27, You ſay, that you do not deny " *the
neceſſity and propriety of ſubjects paying taxes."* But
in not denying this, Sir, do you not indirectly
give up the point ? Do you not grant, that, as
the Coloniſts are not protected by the king alone,
but by the whole legiſlative power of Great Britain, they are not under the juriſdiction of the
king alone, but of *all* the Britiſh legiſlature.
Now if they are not the *ſubjects* of the king, as
unconnected with the Britiſh parliament ; but as conſtitutionally connected with that high court, which
ſup-

fupplies him with proper fubfidies to protect his
American dominions; it is evident that they owe
taxes to the king and the Britifh parliament ; for you
yourfelf acknowledge " *the neceffity of* SUBJECTS *paying taxes*" to the fupreme power which protects them.
But which tax have they, of late, confented to pay ?
Has it been a tax upon tea, or upon ftampt paper ?

Should you reply, that they have offered to pay
taxes to the king and their provincial affemblies, I
reply, that this is not paying capital tribute, to whom
capital tribute IS DUE : For capital tribute is due to
the capital protective power; and the capital power
that protects the Colonifts, is not the king and the
regency of Hanover, or the king and the Irifh parliament, much lefs the king and a provincial affembly ;
but the king and the *Britifh* parliament. Had the
Americans got their wealth under the protection of
the Irifh; had the Hanoverian fleets kept off the
Spanifh fhips from the American coafts ; or had
fquadrons of American men of war beat off the
French fleets; I would not hefitate a moment to
affirm, that the Colonifts ought to pay proportionable taxes to the king and the *Irifh* parliament ; to
the elector and regency of Hanover ; or to the king
of Britifh America and the American affemblies.
But, when all this has been done for the Colonifts
by the king and the *Britifh* parliament, I confefs
to you, Sir, that [fetting afide the confideration of
the {love and duty, which colonies owe to their mother-country.] I cannot fee what law of gratitude,
equity, and juftice the Colonifts can plead, to refufe
paying the king and the *Britifh parliament* moderate
and proportionable taxes.

Page 36, You indirectly appeal to the cafe of
" the patriots of Charles's days," who refufed to
pay the tax called *fhip-money* : But their caufe was
far better than that of the Americans. The fhip-
money was demanded by the king *alone*; but the
king *alone* is not the fupreme legiflative power that
protects the fubjects of Great-Britain, becaufe he
can make no laws and of confequence raife no taxes,
without the concurrence of the parliament. The
pa-

patriots of the laſt century were not then abſolutely bound, either by the law of God, or the law of the land, to pay a tax, which had not the ſanction of the legiſlative power; a money-bill paſſed by the king *alone*, being no law at all according to the Britiſh conſtitution. But a proportionable money-bill, as the ſtamp act,—a bill paſſed by the complete legiſlative power of Great Britain, is every way binding in all the dominions of Great Britain. Whoever reſiſts *ſuch* a law, breaks off with the legiſlative power, affects independence, and commences a petty ſovereign.

I have ſaid that a rightful " ſovereign has a right to live by his noble buſineſs;" and becauſe I have obſerved, that in England the ſovereign, [i. e. the legiſlative, and protective power] is the king and his parliament, you ſuppoſe I have poured ſhame upon the cauſe I defend. " So, &c. [ſay you page 25] " a member of parliament, inſtead of vacating " his ſeat, ought to have a place provided for him " upon his becoming a member of the legiſlature." No, Sir; your inference has no connexion with my doctrine. If you had ſaid, that every member of parliament, while he attends the parliament has a right to a public maintenance ſuitable to his ſhare in the legiſlature; you would have ſaid what I mean, and what no unprejudiced perſon will deny. If the king and parliament ordered that all the attending members ſhall be honourably entertained during the ſeſſion, at the expence of the public: and that a proper ſum ſhall be annually raiſed to diſcharge this expence; what Briton would be ſo niggardly, ungrateful and unjuſt, as to find fault with ſuch a ſtatute? Was our Lord miſtaken when he ſaid, *The labourer is worthy of his hire?* If the ſpeaker, who is the principal member of the houſe of Commons, enjoys, as ſpeaker, an income of ſome thouſand pounds a year, does he not " live by his buſineſs?" Might not all the other members do the ſame in due proportion? When they exempt themſelves and their friends, from paying the tax which we call *poſtage*, do they not ſhew that the legiſlature have pecuniary rights which other Britons have not ? And if their generofity prevents their ufing thofe felf-evident rights, fhould we not extol their difinterednefs, rather than pour contempt upon their reafonable and conftitutional prerogative ?

Unable to invalidate my doctrine by any juft argument, you have recourfe to a polemical ftratagem, which will do your caufe no credit. To render the politics I defend odious to your readers, you infinuate, that upon my principles, the fovereign *" is en-" titled to juft what be pleafes, and may take it with or " without confent, whenever he thinks proper."* This doctrine, which you impute to me, p. 27, has no more connexion with my fyftem, than darknefs with the rifing fun. I abhor it as well as you, Sir; being fully perfuaded, that legiflative power is to be ufed *for good,* and not for evil ; for protection, and not for tyranny. If the king and parliament had laid difproportionable and unreafonable taxes upon our American fellow-fubjects, I would no more have taken the pen in defence of *fuch* taxation, than I would take it in vindication of robbery.

Nor do my appeals to the propriety of giving the lawyers and phyficians whom we employ, the proper fees they demand of us, prove that I hold the doctrine of defpotifm ; for, as I fhould be a *knave* if I refufed to give a gentleman of the faculty a reafonable fee for his attendance ; fo fhould I be a *fool* if I fuppofed, that he *" is entitled to juft what he pleafes."* I only affert, that, as a good man will find a medium between *difhonefty* and *folly,* with refpect to the fees due to his phyfician and lawyer; fo a candid Colonift will find a middle way between the injuftice of the patriots, who refufe moderate taxes to the legiflative power that protects them ; and between the flavifh tamenefs of the poltroons, who fuffer a rapacious tyrant to grind their faces and fuck their blood. Neverthelefs, I dare affirm, that as we truft to a certain degree a lawyer's confcience, an apothecary's difcretion, and a phyfician's candor, with re-

fpect

spect to their bills and fees; we may also trust to a certain degree, the discretion of our governors with respect to their money-bills and taxes. And therefore nothing can be more contrary to good manners, loyalty, reason, and conscience, than to represent the sovereign who protects the Colonists as a *robber* and a *tyrant*, for laying a MODERATE tax upon them, in order to discharge the national debt, and the daily expences of the government.

You indeed insinuate that the case is not parallel, because we employ our physicians and lawyers "*voluntarily*." But have not the Colonists "voluntarily" reaped for an hundred years the benefit of protection from the king and parliament? And, supposing they can now support themselves without British protection; yet are they not guilty of injustice if they *now* refuse to pay proportionable taxes? What would you think of my honesty, if the following case were matter of fact? I "*voluntarily*" employ a lawyer for ten years to recover an estate. When I have gained my ends, he demands fees, which on account of my poverty, he forbore doing before. I storm on the occasion; I run up and down screaming robbery! tyranny! And at last I turn my back upon him with such a speech as this; Sir, I can do without you *now*; and as I am not willing to employ you any more, you have no right to demand fees of me as your DUE. I am a free man, and you shall not treat me as an *abject slave*, by insisting on fees with or *without* my consent." If I put off my industrious lawyer with this American plea, would not your moral feelings brand me as a man devoid of conscience and honour?

I grant however, that the case between the taxes of the sovereign, and the fees of a lawyer, is not exactly similar: But if the parallel fails, it is in a point which does your cause no service. For altho' I am at perfect liberty to dismiss my honest lawyer as soon as I please, when I have paid him his reasonable fees; I cannot cast off the authority of my rightful sove-

reign

reign as foon as I pleafe, when I have paid his reafonable taxes; and I prove it by the following reafons:—(1) I may poffibly live 'fifty years without going to law, but I cannot fafely live one day in fociety without being protected:—(2) As an *unconnected* individual, I may neglect the care of my property as I pleafe; and if a man unjuftly demands my cloak, I may let him have my coat alfo: But, as a man joined with others in civil fociety, I am a debtor to all the fociety with which I am connected: I muft defend my property as a part of the common ftock; and of confequence, I muft pay taxes, and help to fupport the fovereign, who protects and guards the whole fociety. Hence it is, that thofe who live in the centre of the kingdom, pay as much towards the fleet as thofe that live on the fea coaft; though they are not half fo much expofed to the depredations of invaders and pirates.—(3) The laws of God and of the land bind me to obey *my* rightful fovereign rather than *another* king, in all things which are juft and reafonable: But none of thefe laws bind me to employ one lawyer rather than another, under the fearful penalties due to *rebellion* and *high treafon.* If the American patriots confidered this, would they not blufh to infinuate, that we may change our fovereigns as we do our tradefmen; and that, as the Colonifts no longer demand the protection of Great-Britain, the Britifh legiflature has no longer any right to demand taxes of them? Who could fufficiently wonder at the infolence and injuftice of the following plea, which, I fuppofe, is urged by Yorkfhire non-voters. Neither we, nor our county, are reprefented in parliament according to our wifhes. We We are not afraid of an invafion. Yorkfhire is large and populous. We can protect ourfelves: And therefore we refufe to pay any thing towards the protection of the Britifh dominions. *What we have is* ABSOLUTELY *our own:* Nor will we be robbed by any body; no not by the legiflature. For, as we are defirous, that the fovereign would keep his protection

tection to himself; so are we determined to keep
our money to ourselves." I question, Sir, if prejudiced as you are in favour of the American patriots,
you would not be one of the first, to exclaim against
such Yorkshire patriots.

Nor do you weaken my argument taken from the
proper fees due to lawyers, by intimating, that such
fees are " LAWFUL, ACCUSTOMED *fees,*" and that
" *In England the Sovereign has no power to recover a*
debt even for himself, but according to LAW" Has it
not been in all ages, and in all parts of the world,
the " *custom*" of civiliz'd nations to pay taxes to the
protective power they are under? Is it not the
" *custom*" of all just sovereigns, to lay those taxes according to the wants and emergencies of the government? When such taxes are properly laid by the
supreme power which makes and executes every law,
are they not " *lawful?*" Is it not " *according to*
law," that the king and parliament laid a little tax
upon our American fellow-subjects? And are there
no statutes enjoining, that the goods of perverse subjects, who refuse to pay lawful and reasonable taxes,
shall be distrained ; and that, if such subjects oppose
the distraint, they shall be farther proceeded against
according to law; especially if instead of paying
taxes, they break into ships, and tyrannically destroy
the property of their fellow-subjects?

If these observations overthrow your reply to the
rational arguments, by which I have supported the
doctrine of taxation laid down in the Calm Address ;
I may consider,

SECONDLY, how you answer my SCRIPTURAL
arguments, on which, as a *Christian,* I lay the *great-*
est stress.

Page, 52, you say, " The golden rule of scrip-
" ture both for governors and governed, is this :
" As YE WOULD *that men should do unto you,* DO YE
" EVEN SO *unto them.* Now I presume the good
                                            " people

" people of England *would not* be willing that the
" Americans, in their affemblies, fhould tax *Englifh*
" *property* here : and why fhould we therefore de-
" fire, in our parliament, to tax *American property*
" there ?"

I reply: The cafe is not fimilar. The Americans are *protected*, and the Britifh legiflature is the
protecting power. The protected owe taxes to their
protectors, and not the protectors to the protected.
You apply " the golden rule of the fcripture" to
the cafe in hand, as unfortunately as I fhould do,
if I faid, that this rule intitles my fervant to command me, becaufe I have a right to command him :
and that I may *juftly* demand a fee of the phyfician
who attends me, becaufe he *juftly* demands a fee of
me for his attendance. Nay, if your argument is
juft, it proves that the king is bound to pay *you*
taxes. You may go to his majefty, and addrefs him
thus, according to your patriotic doctrine; O king,
*the golden rule of fcripture, both for governors and go-
verned*, obliges thee to do to *me*, as thou *wouldft* that
I *fhould* do to *thee*. Now, thou wouldft that I fhould
pay *thee* taxes, and therefore, drop thy Britifh partiality, commence an American patriot, and confefs
that thou fhouldft pay *me* taxes.

If the objection, which you draw from our Lord's
golden rule, is trifling; may not that which you
raife from his bleffed example, be affirmed to be deplorable? Our reformers fay, in their *homily againft
wilful rebellion*, Part ii. ' No EXAMPLE ought to
' be of more force with us chriftians, than the
' example of Chrift our mafter, who, tho' he were
' the Son of God, yet did always behave himfelf
' moft reverently to fuch men as were in authority
' in the world in his time. He behaved not himfelf
' *rebellioufly*; but openly did teach the Jews to *pay*
' *tribute* to the Roman emperor, tho' a foreign and
' a pagan prince : yea, himfelf with his apoftles paid
' tribute unto him.' How different is your doctrine
from that of thofe loyal champions of truth ! That
very

very example of our Lord's *loyalty*, which they fo-
highly extol, you [indirectly] reprefent as an inftance of *weaknefs*. " *How could he*" [fay you,
p. 54] " *avoid paying the tribute demanded of him ?*"
So, it feems that our Lord paid tribute becaufe he
could not *avoid* paying it ! He did it thro' *neceffity !*
He broke his own commandments delivered by St.
Peter and St. Paul ! *Submit yourfelves to every ordinance of man* FOR THE LORD's SAKE ;—*Ye muft be
fubject not only for wrath, but alfo for* CONSCIENCE
SAKE. Fear of wrath, and human prudence, were
the flavifh motives of his loyal action ! Nay, you
intimate, p. 55, that he thought it lawful to pay
tribute to Cæfar, only in the fame fenfe in which it
is " *lawful to give a highwayman our money*," and
p. 54, you roundly affert, that " *Such a*" [forced]
" *fubmiffion as this, is all the fubmiffion our Lord's* EX-
" AMPLE *can be fuppofed in the leaft to countenance.*"

If you could prove this affertion, Sir, the bright-
nefs of our Lord's moral character would fuffer a
total eclipfe. For, if " what a man has is *abfolutely* his own ;" and if the Roman emperor had
not, as protector of the Jews, a reafonable claim
to their tribute-money, did not our Lord prevari-
cate, and was not an untruth found in his mouth,
when he faid to the Jews, who fhewed him the
tribute-money, *Render therefore to Cæfar the things
which* ARE *Cæfar's?* In what fenfe could he fay,
that this money was CÆSAR'S, if Cæfar had no
more right to it than an highwayman ? And with
what moral propriety could he bid the Jews to
RENDER fuch money to Cæfar, as a part of Cæfar's
PROPERTY ?

This is not all : The manner, in which our
Lord enforced paying taxes to Tiberius, fhews that
he refted this branch of our duty to our neighbour
upon the very fame authority, on which he refted
our obedience to God himfelf. To be convinced
of it, we need only confider his evangelical charge,
Render therefore to CÆSAR, *the things which* ARE
C.ÆSAR'S ;

CÆSAR's; *and to* GOD, *the things which* ARE
GOD's. The manner in which the two parts of
this injunction are connected, demonstrates, that we
must pay taxes to the civil power by which we are
protected, as conscientiously as we pay adoration to
the divine power by which we exist. But, according to your patriotic doctrine, our Lord's solemn
precept degenerates into a charge as absurd and pro-
fane as the following: " Your money is *absolutely*
" your own; render it therefore to Cæsar, or to an
" highwayman, for it is his if he demands it: nor
" forget in like manner, to render your all to God:
" for it is his, as your money is an highwayman's."
What monstrous doctrines does your patriotism cou-
ple together! *Geminantur tigribus agni!* And how
hard is it to do justice to scripture, when we directly
or indirectly part these inseparable precepts, *Fear
God and honour the king,* i. e. the protective power:
Honour him with a reasonable part of *thy substance,* as
well as by thy respectful behaviour!

Let us see if you are more successful in your
attempt to overthrow what you call my " *grand
plea from scripture, taken from* Rom. xlii." S. Paul
there proves by various reasons, that taxes are due
to *the higher powers* that protect us. Such powers
are ordained of God:—Resisting them, when they
lay reasonable taxes upon us, is *resisting the ordinance
of God:—Those who resist,* in such a case, *shall receive
to themselves damnation:—They are God's ministers to
us* FOR GOOD; their grand business being to protect
us in the way of virtue, and to curb or punish us in
the way of vice:—and *they attend continually to this
very thing,* i. e. to our protection when we do well,
and to our punishment when we break the laws.
RENDER *therefore to all their* DUES, *tribute to whom
tribute is* DUE, &c.

To set aside the force of this nervous comment
of St. Paul upon the words of our Lord, RENDER
unto Cæsar, &c. you tell us p. 63, that " *the apostle
" does not take upon him in the least, to determine* TO
" WHOM

" WHOM *tribute was due.*" But are you not miftaken, Sir? Does he not explicitly fay *to whom,*
when he mentions *the higher powers* that protect us?
Now if the king and the Britifh parliament are
the higher powers, that have hitherto protected the
Colonies; does not the apoftle decide our controverfy, as much as if he faid, Let the American
Colonies pay taxes to the king and parliament, who
are *the higher powers* that have *continually attended* to
the protection of the Colonifts when they did well,
and now attend to the punifhing of them, becaufe
they do ill?

But you add alfo, " *The apoftle does not take*
" *upon him to determine what* QUANTUM *of tribute*
" *might be due.*" True: for he did not *attend continually* to the dangers of the ftate, and to the beft
means of averting them. He minded his own bufinefs, inftead of reflecting upon the higher powers
in the execution of theirs. He knew no more than
you, and I, what expence thofe powers might be
at, to protect him and all his fellow-fubjects; tho'
he could eafily conceive, that fuch expence was pro-
digious, fince *the chief captain Lyfias* employed once
an army to refcue him from the rage of mobbing religionifts; and protected him on another occafion, by
granting him a guard of 200 *foldiers,* 70 *horfemen,*
and 200 *fpearmen:* Acts xxiii. 23, 27. Now as *Paul*
did not know, but myriads of his fellow-fubjects
ftood in need of fuch a guard as well as himfelf, and
as he did not claim a place in the legiflature *jure di-
vino,* he did not pretend to determine the *quantum* of
tribute neceffary to maintain a fufficient, protecting
force, all over the Roman empire. But what has
this to do with the queftion? Could not *Paul* make
Chriftians underftand that they muft pay rent to
their landlords, and taxes to the higher powers,
without " *determining the quantum*" of fuch rents and
taxes? Muft not a divine, who makes fo frivolous an
objection, be at a ftrange lofs for arguments?

But

But you go on: p. 63, The apoftle only enjoins
" the confcientious payment of what was due, to
" thofe to whom it was due, according to *the nature*
" *of the government under which they lived.*" True,
Sir, if by *the nature of the government under which
we live*, you mean the reafonable demands of the
legiflative power which protects us. But if you
mean by this phrafe, as your fcheme requires, that
we are to pay taxes only according to the nice fpecu-
lations of men, who cry up the conftitution one hour,
and decry it the next, if it does not fuit their chime-
rical notions of equal reprefentation, and their
injudicious ideas of liberty ; your doctrine is fub-
verfive of the apoftle's loyal precept, opens the door
to all manner of fedition, and leaves Chriftians at an
utter uncertainty with refpect to a capital branch of
morality, the payment of taxes : And I prove my
affertion by the following obfervations.

(1) The Jews were divided among themfelves,
with refpect to *the nature of the government they were
under.* While fome of them faid, We are under the
Roman government ; *We will have no king but Cæfar*;
the patriots faid, " *We were never in bondage to any
man*; we are freemen; we are under the Mofaic
conftitution ; we owe no taxes to Cæfar. To pay
taxes to an heathen prince is to give up the excellent
conftitution which our anceftors have tranfmitted to
us." Now, in full oppofition to thefe plaufible notions, our Lord bid the Jews pay taxes to Cæfar,
according to the Roman government ; another government this, than that which the patriots faid they
were under.

(2) When Jofeph and the virgin Mary went to
Bethlehem, to be taxed according to the decree of
Cæfar Auguflus ; the ableft politicians were at a lofs
to fay what was precifely the *nature* of the Roman
government, which the Jews and moft other nations
were then under ; fo many were the changes which
it had undergone. At firft it was a monarchy, by
and by a republic, headed by confuls, and by and by
a republic

a republic headed by a dictator. One time the fupreme power had centered in a decemvirate; at
another time a triumvirate had held the reins of adminiſtration. At that juncture the government wore
the form of a monarchy again; but there was yet
a conſiderable minority, who held the high, republican principles of Cato, Brutus, and Caſſius, the three
great patriots of the day. This minority conſidered
Cæſar Auguſtus as a tyrant, and a robber, to whom
no taxes were due; aſſerting that the government,
which the Romans were under, was entirely republican. Now, what muſt ſubjects do in ſuch a caſe?
Muſt they refuſe to pay taxes to the power that
actually protects them, till the minority and thema-
jority are perfectly agreed concerning *" the nature of
the government under which they live?"* Or muſt
they loſe their time in trying to decide nice, political queſtions, which puzzle the men who have
ſtudied civil law all their life?

(3) As it was next to impoſſible, to determine
with exactneſs, what was the nature of the *Roman*
government; ſo it requires more wiſdom, than millions of people in the Britiſh empire are maſters of,
preciſely to determine the nature of the *Britiſh* government. The ſtrong Whigs are for the republican government, which obtained in the days of
Cromwell and the rump. The ſtrong Tories contend for the high, monarchical government, which
prevailed in the days of king James II. You and
I, Sir, are for the government, which has obtained
ſince the revolution. Nor are you ſatisfied even
with this; for you ſpeak of *an avowed defect in the
preſent conſtitution.* You are for an equal repreſentation of the people, that is, for an utter impoſſibi-
lity: and p. 98, you inform us, " That, till the
" eighth year of Henry the VI, all the reſidents in
" a county were permitted to elect repreſentatives,
" without exception;" inſinuating, that now " *the
" repreſentation here in England is imperfect,*" becauſe
that practice is diſuſed. Now, Sir, if this kind of

B   repre-

representation is effential to *the nature of the government we live under*; and if we are not bound to pay taxes, which are not laid according to that ancient form of the conftitution; it is clear, that no man in Great Britain is bound to pay any tax at all : for no tax is laid according to your levelling fcheme of reprefentation, and according to *the nature of the government*, which obtained before Henry VI. Hence it appears, that, as the Pope's bulls formerly loofed Britons from the oaths of fidelity, which they had taken to their fovereign, and by this means raifed and fomented rebellions. So your political refinements loofe not only the Colonies, but Great Britain alfo, from the obligation of paying taxes to the king and parliament. So true it is, that overdoing is the way of undoing; and that *your politics* tend to kindle the flame of rebellion in England, and to keep it up in America. I fay *your politics*, becaufe candor obliges me to do juftice to your good meaning, and to make a friendly diftinction between your perfon and your opinions.

(4) Should you fay, that, though it cannot be expected, that every fubject fhall ftudy the *nature* of all the wheels and fprings, which compofe that piece of political mechanifm, we call *The conftitution*; yet every fubject may chufe his own reprefentative, whofe bufinefs is to decide what taxes muft be paid, according to the conftitution; I reply, that, in moft Chriftian governments, the people are not allowed to chufe any reprefentatives, and therefore in fuch ftates every individual muft, upon your plan, revolt or *perfonally* ftudy politics, that he may know how to pay taxes, according to the *nature* of the conftitution.

Things, I grant, are upon another footing in England. But this does not remove the difficulty : for [not to mention, that perhaps nineteen fubjects in England out of twenty, cannot chufe reprefentatives] the members of parliament are as much divided among themfelves, as the Romans were in the
days

days of Auguſtus, and the Jews in the days of Tiberius. The minority declare, that the Coloniſts are taxed *againſt the nature* of the conſtitution; whilſt the majority aſſert, that they are *conſtitutionally* taxed. Thus your patriotic comment abſolutely unnerves St. Paul's doctrine of taxation, and leaves Chriſtians in the greateſt uncertainty, with reſpect to the payment of taxes, which are the ſinews of government. For, if that payment be ſuſpended on our *notions* of the nature of the government we are under, it might as well be ſuſpended on the *ſhape* of the clouds, and the *colour* of a pigeon's neck.

Should you reply, that, when our repreſentatives do not agree touching the nature of the government we live under, we muſt follow the majority; I anſwer, that the majority has decided the queſtion. But what care ſome patriots for the majority? Does not Americanus openly oppoſe their deciſions, and wiſhfully quote the miſapply'd ſaying, " *Dulce pro patria mori* ;" juſt as if *mori pro pertinacia* was the ſame thing as *pro patria mori ?* O Sir, if the former is ſweet, the latter is the quinteſſence of bitterneſs: for the ſcripture declares, that wilful *rebellion is as the ſin of witchcraft*, and that *ſtubbornneſs is as iniquity and idolatry*.

We have ſeen by what arguments you have endeavoured to prove, that the doctrine of taxation eſpouſed by the ſovereign is *irrational*, and *unſcriptual*. Let us ſee,

THIRDLY, How you attempt to prove, that it is UNCONSTITUTIONAL.

Permit me, Sir, to lay this doctrine before you with ſome capital improvements. The king and parliament believe, that the conſtitution allows of *indirect* repreſentation, and that among the ſeveral ſorts of *indirect* repreſentation, ſome are *leſs* and others *more* indirect. This ſentiment is founded on the fol-

lowing

lowing FACTS. (1) Tho' the conftitution allows a woman, for inftance Queen Elizabeth or Queen Ann, to be the head of the legiflative power, yet no woman-fubject can have any fhare in the legiflature; but all women are indirectly reprefented by the men; be their rank ever fo high, and their property ever fo confiderable.—(2) According to the conftitution, all the voters, who actually chufe parliament-men, indirectly reprefent all the voters who do not, or cannot attend the election; whether the abfent voters be at home or abroad, in jails or on fick-beds. —(3) Tho' the number of the non-voters exceeds ten or twenty times the number of the voters; yet, according to the conftitution, the voters indirectly reprefent the countlefs body of the non-voters, whether fuch non-voters be poor men of age, or rich men under age.— (4) The conftitution allows that men of a certain profeffion fhall be particularly reprefented, when men of other honourable profeffions are not. Thus the clergy are *particularly* reprefented, when the rich body of our merchants, the gentlemen of the law, thofe of the fleet, thofe of the army, and thofe of the faculty, are not allowed a *particular* reprefentation. This conftitutional partiality does not ftop here: The *whole order* of bifhops is admitted into the houfe of *lords*; but not one feat in the houfe of commons, is appropriated to the order of the priefts. Such is the latitude which the conftitution allows herfelf, when fhe decides concerning the right of reprefentation!—(5) According to the fame prerogative, fhe orders, that the little county of Rutlandfhire, fhall fend as many members as the large county of Yorkfhire; fo that if Yorkfhire is ten times more populous than Rutlandfhire, the reprefentation of a Yorkfhire freeholder is by ten degrees weaker or *lefs direct*, than the reprefentation of a Rutlandfhire freeholder. And, fuppofe the city of Briftol contains a thoufand times more freemen, than the decay'd borough of old Sarum, the conftitution allows, that a burgefs of old Sarum fhall be a thoufand times *more directly*, or *particularly* reprefented than a freeman of Briftol.—(6.) On the fame plan, fome flourifhing and

and populous towns are not allow'd to fend any reprefentative, when fome poor and deferted Cornifh
or Welch boroughs, fend as many members as fome
of the greateſt cities in the kingdom.—(7) The conſtitution allows, that the prefent members fhall reprefent all thofe who are abfent; that the majority of
the prefent members, fhall indirectly reprefent the
minority; and that the parliament fhall determine
the affairs of all the Britifh fettlements in Europe,
Afia, Africa, and in the Weſt-Indies; altho' the
Coloniſts fettled in thofe parts have no direct reprefentatives in parliament: I fay *no direct reprefentatives* becaufe the conſtitution fuppofes, that as the
men *indirectly* reprefent all the women; the burgeffes, all that are not burgeffes; and the freeholders,
all that have no freehold; and as the majority in
parliament *indirectly* reprefents the minority, and the
members who are in the houfe *indirectly* reprefent
thofe who are abfent; fo the three branches of the
legiflature, indirectly reprefent all the political body
which is called the Britifh empire, juſt as the head,
the heart, and the breaft indirectly reprefent all the
natural body; whether the hands and feet touch each
other, or whether they are widely extended towards
the eaſt and the weſt.—(8) The profperity of the
mother-country being as clofely connected with the
profperity of the Colonies, as the welfare of parents
is connected with that of their children, Great Britain has as rational and natural a right to reprefent
the Colonies, as parents have to reprefent their children; prefent burgeffes, thofe that are abfent; and
voting free-holders, thofe that have no vote.—Laſtly,
matter of fact demonſtrates, that the American Colonies are *indirectly* reprefented in parliament, and matter of fact bears down ten thoufand fophifms. I
have already made appear, that the conſtitution allows of various degrees of indirect reprefentation,
fome proximate, and others more remote. And, that
the Coloniſts are reprefented in one of the degrees
which the conſtitution allows, appears by the fol-

lowing

lowing remark : As a lawyer, who pleads your
caule in a court of judicature, is indirectly your
reprefentative, whether you chofe him or not: So
the members, who plead the caufe of the Colonifts
in the high court of Parliament, fhew themfelves
the indirect reprefentatives of the Colonifts, whether the Colonifts chofe them or not. And therefore, to deny that the Provincials are indirectly reprefented in parliament, is as bold an impofition upon the good fenfe of the public, as to deny that the
minority in both houfes of parliament oppofes the
claims of Great Britain and votes for the Colonies :
For reafon, confcience, and the conftitution agree
to decide, that if the Colonifts are not indirectly
reprefented in parliament, the members, who plead
their caufe, have no more right to vote for them
than you and I have. My demonftration is fhort:
A confiderable number of parliament-men vote in
both houfes, that parliamentary taxation is unjuft
with refpect to the Colonies ; all the members have
a right to vote in their favour, and would do it, if
their confcience permitted ; and therefore the Colonifts are incontestably, tho' indirectly, reprefented
in parliament. Nor can one of the members, who
compofe the minority, *give his vote for the Americans*, without confuting himfelf, if he denies that
they are *indirectly* reprefented in the parliament :
and if they are indirectly reprefented in the parliament, they may be CONSTITUTIONALLY taxed BY
THE PARLIAMENT. On this ground, which is firm
as *matter of fact*, the majority are ready to ftand the
minority and you, in all the courts of reafon, which
are or can be erected in Great Britain or America.

Confider we now what you object to this *conftitutional* doctrine. Page 37, you fay, " The non-
" voters here can point out their *virtual* reprefen-
" tatives, as clearly as the voters can point out their
" *direct* reprefentatives. But who are the fpecific
" virtual reprefentatives of America ? Who are
" appointed to reprefent the property there ?" I
reply :

reply : (1) The whole body, in which the legiſlative power is lodged, is appointed by the conſtitution to protect the property of all the ſubjects of Great Britain. (2) Your ideas of repreſentation are far too much circumſcribed. Though the members of a Corniſh borough *directly* repreſent the burgeſſes of that borough, yet they *indirectly* repreſent the commons of all England, and of all the Britiſh dominions. If it were not ſo, they could have no voice in the houſe, except when the petty concerns of their borough are debated. Now Sir, by the ſame conſtitutional rule, by which the members of a Welch borough are appointed to manage the affairs of all England; the members of Middleſex are appointed to manage the affairs of all Britiſh America. And if you want me to point out ſome of the *indirect, virtual repreſentatives* of the Americans, I take up the firſt news-paper, and point at the names of the members, who diſtinguiſh themſelves by their zeal to ſupport what they judge to be the rights of the Americans. And I aſk, If theſe Lords and Gentlemen do not *indirectly* repreſent the rich and the poor in our colonies, what right have they to vote for the Coloniſts more than the members of the Iriſh Parliament ?

Page 31, You intimate, that it is " perfectly un-
" conſtitutional, to exclude the Americans from
" having a voice in the diſpoſal of their property,
" whoſe eſtates may amount to thirty-nine pounds
" per annum ;" though you grant, that " a man
" in England can have no voice in the diſpoſal of
" his property, whoſe eſtate amounts to no more
" than thirty-nine ſhillings per annum." But have
you forgot, that the conſtitution allows " the pot-
" boilers in the deſpicable hovels of ſome boroughs"
to have votes for parliament-men, while ſome "*free-*
" *holders in Gloceſter, Hereford, and London, have*
" *no votes for town or county,*" becauſe they are neither freemen nor liverymen. On this important
conceſſion, which you make page 98, I reſt the fol-

lowing queries. If the conſtitution allows the tax
ation of ſome FREEHOLDERS in the cities of *Gloceſter,*
Hereford, and *London*; although ſuch freeholders
through an accidental cauſe, HAVE NO VOTES FOR
TOWN OR COUNTY; why can it not allow the taxation of ſome FREEHOLDERS, who, through an accidental cauſe, have no votes for England or America? And if you grant, that the conſtitution permits, that ſome men, who poſſeſs a FREEHOLD in
the center of Great Britain, are *conſtitutionally* taxed
by the parliament, though they have no vote; do
you not expoſe your prejudice before all the world,
if you ſay that the Coloniſts cannot be *conſtitutionally*
taxed by the parliament, merely becauſe they have
no vote?

I have preſſed you with the caſe of ſome members
of parliament, who are conſtitutionally taxed with
or *without* their conſent, ſo long as they chuſe to
live abroad. P. 31, 32, you reply, " The Americans are *at home:*" You inſinuate, that my doctrine ſuppoſes they " are NEVER AT HOME," and
you humouroully ſay, " Were I a Coloniſt, the
" prerogative I would humbly ſue for, ſhould be
" that of being permitted to be *at home*; for home
" is home, ſays the old proverb, be it ever ſo home-
" ly." I anſwer, Lord Pigot, a member of parliament, who is in the Eaſt Indies, and Mr. Hancock, a member of the congreſs, have the full leave
of the conſtitution to be AT HOME. Only it muſt
be remembered, that, by emigration, they have
their home in two places; as the gentlemen who
have a houſe in London, and another in the country. They have their *legiſlative* home in Great
Britain, and their *actual* home, Lord Pigot in Ben-
gal, and Mr. Hancock in Philadelphia. If they
will enjoy the prerogatives of their *legiſlative* home,
they muſt return to England, juſt as the gentlemen,
who will fill their ſeats in the parliament, and enjoy
their honours at court, muſt leave their country-
ſeats and repair to London. Nor ſay that the diftinction

tinction I make between our *actual* and our *legislative* home is frivolous; for Dr. Price, your oracle, says, " *They* [the colonies] *gloried in their relation* " *to us;—and they always spoke of* THIS *country and* " *looked to it as* THEIR HOME." Now, as the Colonists were never so destitute of good sense, as to look on England as their *actual* home; it remains, that your oracle has spoken nonsense, or that England is their *principal*, *legislative* home. - And would to God, they were not grown so uneasy, as to despise this " home, be it ever so homely"!

You hint indeed at the inconveniency and impossibility of the Colonists coming back to their legislative home; but this objection makes as much against your scheme of representation as against ours; for you insinuate, that all the non-voters in England may go and settle in the few Boroughs, where the constitution allows every pot-boiler to be a voter; and you give us a hint, that if they do not, " it is their own fault." But is it not more practicable for all the Free-holders in America, to crowd into Great Britain; than for all the non-voters in Great Britain, to crowd into such privileged boroughs as you speak of; or for all the women, who have freeholds in England, to change their sex, that they may have a vote at the next election?

You reply, p. 38, " The representation in ENG- " LAND is *unequal*, owing to a great variety of ca- " sual circumstances, which it would be useless to " enumerate." Now, Sir, applying to all the British empire, what you say of England, I answer, The representation with respect to AMERICA is " *unequal*; owing to a great variety of casual cir- " cumstances," such as emigration, distance, interposing seas, and the impropriety of multiplying * parliaments, which would as much weaken the
                    B 5   empire,

empire, as you would do a piece of clock-work,
if you contrived to make each wheel move by means
of a separate spring. Thus, if I am not mistaken,
your own conceſſions, backed by one of *Dr.
Price's obſervations*, ſhew that, ſo far, your attempt to demonſtrate that the parliamentary doctrine of taxation
is contrary to the conſtitution, only ſhews that it is
TRULY CONSTITUTIONAL.

Come we now to your *capital argument*, the firſt
part of which runs thus: " *The American* CAN
" *have no voice in the diſpoſal of his property; and
" what is worſe, thoſe who are to have the power
" of diſpoſing of it, are under every poſſible tempta-
" tion to abuſe that power, becauſe every ſhilling they
" take out of the pocket of an American is ſo much
" ſaved in their own.*" To this I reply, *Vind*. p.
33, ' You miſtake: For as many of the Coloniſts as
' chuſe to purchaſe a freehold in England, MAY
' become electors; and as many as have a ſuffici-
' ent fortune MAY be candidates at the next elec-
' tion;' adding, that you yourſelf ſpeak of a
" *late American candidate, who was a friend to
" America.*" But you take no notice of this *ſufficient* anſwer.

Preſſing you ſtill farther, I remind you that
' There are ſeveral members in both houſes of par-
' liament, who have a very large property in Ame-
' rica, and who, when they tax the Coloniſts, take
' far more money out of their own pocket than
' they

---

in mechanics; the more a government and a machine are need-
leſſly complicated, the weaker is their motion, and the greater the
danger of their being out of order. It is the glory and ſtrength
of our conſtitution to be compact, *in ſe totus teres atque rotundus.*
As I could not admire an human body with one head and a dozen
ſtomachs, I could not be pleaſed to ſee Great Britain and her Colonies exhibiting to the world a political body, with one royal head
and a dozen ſupreme courts of parliament. If ſuch needleſs diviſions and multiplications do not tend to ſpeedy diſſolution, they
certainly do to weakneſs, confuſion, ſlowneſs of operation, and a
thouſand evils, which France with her ſeveral unconnected parliaments ſo ſeverely feels.

' they probably do out of the pocket of Mr. Han-
' cock.' To this you reply, page 41, " *But what
" fecurity have the Americans, that there will al-
" ways be fuch members in parliament?*" I anfwer:
They have the faine fecurity for it, which we have
that there will always be a prince to fill the throne,
and a number of peers to compofe an houfe of
Lords. It is not impoffible, that a plague fhould
fweep away all the royal family, and all the nobility;
but would it be right, to diftrefs the public upon
fuch a fuppofition? Would it not be ridiculous to
frighten the fimple, by telling them that the conftitution is in danger, and that, as we *have no fecurity*
that all the royal family and all the nobility will not
die of the plague, or be blown up by a fecond gun-
powder plot, " *our conftitution is almoft loft,*" and we
are likely to have foon another rump parliament
without king and without houfe of Lords?

But you add: " *Unlefs all the members of the Bri-
" tifh parliament had American property, they would
" not be on a level with the non-voters in England.*"
I reply: If the American Colonies are, as fome patriots fuppofe, the capital fpring of Britifh wealth, all
the members of parliament have a particular, tho'
indirect concern in the profperity of the Colonifts;
nor does the conftitution require that taxed fubjects
fhould be on a level with each other *in every poffible
refpect.* The Americans fhould be thankful for being
on a level, not only with the non-voters in England,
in the important right of qualifying themfelves to be
voters, or candidates for feats in parliament; but
alfo with the free-holders in London, who have no
vote, and with the members of parliament abroad,
who, through emigration, cannot *actually* fhare in
the legiflature. I repeat it, to attempt to bring
about a reprefentation equal *in every refpect*, is as abfurd as to attempt making all our fellow-fubjects of
one fize, one age, one fex, one country, one revenue,
one rank, and one capacity.

　　　Another

Another of my anfwers to your grand argument ran thus : ‘ It is improbable that our law-givers ‘ would fave a dirty fhilling in their pocket, by op- ‘ preffively taking one out of an American's pocket. ‘ Being men of fortune they are raifed by their cir- ‘ cumftances above the felonious trick you fpeak of.’ Page 40, you humouroufly reply, “ I fuppofe, Sir, “ if you fhould lend a few thoufands to any of our “ legiflators, you would not pretend to afk for a *bond*. “ It would be *ungenerous* to fufpect men of fuch cir- “ cumftances as the conftitution obliges all our law- “ givers to be, of fuch a *felonious trick* as not paying “ you again.” But this reply of yours is fully ob- viated by my fifth anfwer, which is as follows : ‘ If ‘ the Colonifts were afraid of being taxed more hea- ‘ vily than the rule of proportion allows, fhould they ‘ not have humbly requefted, that the parliament ‘ would fettle the matter by an ACT,’—or “ a BOND which might have been an effectual check upon the abufe of the power of taxation ?

You think to unnerve this anfwer by faying, p. 42, “ What the Colonifts *fhould* have done is one “ thing, and what the Britifh parliament *has done* is “ another.” True: The parliament has laid upon the Colonifts a little tax, and they have revolted, in- ftead of paying it with the loyalty which becomes good fubjects, and with the prudence which becomes men jealous of their liberty ; and therefore their con- duct is unjuftifiable, and that of the parliament rea- fonable. You farther infinuate, that, as you are not obliged to “ *conform to the eftablifhed church*,” fo the Colonifts were not obliged to fubmit to Britifh taxation in the prudential manner I have men- tioned. But the cafe is not parallel. Neither chriftianity nor the conftitution obliges us to con- form to the eftablifhed church ; whereas both en- join us to *render to all their* DUES, *tribute to whom tribute is* DUE, that is, to the fupreme protective power.

You

You have another string to your bow : Sensible
that the preceding argument is not strong enough
to shoot the arrow of conviction into a thinking
man's breast, you add, p. 42. " A man that robs
" me on the highway, may think that I *should* have
" previously asked him if he did not want my
" money.—but I presume this will not justify his
" robbing me." So, Sir, you will always insinuate, that we are no more bound to pay reasonable
taxes to the legislative power which protects us,
than we are bound to give our money to a robber
who demands it! But when Americanus argues in
this manner, does he not contradict St. Paul, Jesus
Christ, and Mr. Evans himself, who [p. 27.] not
only grants " *the necessity of subjects paying taxes*,"
but intimates that a man who *denies the propriety* of
that custom, and the ground of that propriety, is
" *one of the most unreasonable beings in the universe*,
" *and a mere political Quixote ?*" It does not become me to decide how far you have drawn your
own picture in this candid concession : But, as
you finish your answer to my argument by this display of your consistency, I may desire the public
to judge, whether your reply gives a finishing
stroke to the cause of the parliament, or to your
own.

The other part of your capital argument runs
thus : The Britons who have no vote, or who are
unable to vote by emigration, may " consent to
" the disposal of their property, because they have
" always *this security*, that those who take an ac-
" tive part in the disposal of their property, must
" at the same time dispose of an equal proportion
" of their own." I have already shewn, that the
Colonists have considerable degrees of *security*, that
the parliament will not tax them *disproportionably*.
And if they had properly asked a *fuller* security,
instead of flying to arms, the parliament would undoubtedly have granted their request. But, without
dwelling upon this answer ; to overthrow your argument I need only observe, that it is inconclusive,
because

becaufe it can be retorted, and faps the foundation of what you call " *the fundamental privilege*" of the commons, which is, that no money-bills can reafonably " *originate but from themfelves.*" For, if money-bills always originated from the *Lords*, who are richer than the populace, the commons would *have always this fecurity, that* the Lords in *taking an active part in the difpofal of the people's property, mujl at the fame time difpofe of an equal proportion of their own.* So eafily can your grand argument be turned againft your own caufe! And fo great is the inconfiftency of a fyftem, one part of which you cannot fupport without totally undermining the other!

If thefe remarks recommend themfelves to your *reafon, piety,* and *fober patriotifm*; I hope, Sir, you will confefs, that truth is a file, which we bite in vain; that it is as imprudent to attack a good argument in the field of controverfy, as to lay hold of an antagonift's fword with a naked hand in a field of battle; that your reply has given me an opportunity of *confirming* my Vindication; and that the doctrine of taxation embraced by the parliament is truly *rational, fcriptural,* and *conftitutional.* Q. E. D.

I am,

Rev. Sir,

Your friendly Opponent, and

Obedient Servant in the Gofpel,

J. F.

L E T.

LETTER II.

Rev. Sir,

I Would have taken my leave of you in the preceding letter, had I not confidered, that a patient controvertift ought to contend for Truth, till fhe enjoys her full liberty. The truth I defend is not yet free. She is ftill bound, with three or four of the chains you have loaded her with. Nor can I complete my refcue, without breaking them with my polemical hammer.

I. The firft of thefe chains is your error (or that of Lord Camden) concerning the AESOLUTENESS OF OUR PROPERTY.

Page 34, you ftill infinuate, that " *What a man* " *has is* ABSOLUTELY *his own.*" Neverthelefs, preffed by my objection, you indirectly grant, that *God* has a right to our property. But if *God* has a right to our property, does he not delegate this right to our political *gods*, I mean to our Lawgivers and Governors, who are his *lieutenants* and *reprefentatives?* And in this cafe, how can you fay that NO MAN has a right to take our property from us without our confent; our property being *abfolutely* our own? I ftill farther affert, that, fo long as we live in fociety, our property is a part of the commonwealth: But if it is ABSOLUTELY *our own*, how can it be *a part of the* COMMONWEALTH? And if it is *a part of the* COMMONWEALTH, how can it be ABSOLUTELY our own?
I fup-

I fupport this dilemma by the following Queries.
Who is fuch a novice in politics as not to know,
that private intereft, in a thoufand cafes, is to
yield to public good; and, of confequence *private*
poffeffion to *public* claims? If a man has a thoufand bufhels of wheat, which he hoards up in time
of fcarcity, may he not be juftly compelled to fell
it at a reafonable price, tho' he and his reprefentative fhould cry out ever fo loud, " Oppreffion !
tyrranny ! robbery?"—If a nobleman found rich
mines of coals in his eftate near London, could he
not be legally hindred from working thofe mines,
left the New-caftle colliers, and a thoufand failors
fhould ftarve for want of employment?—If Briftol
were befieged, and you had a houfe near the walls,
where the enemy might lodge his forces to annoy
the city; might not your houfe be juftly pulled
down; tho' you and your American reprefentative
fhould refufe your confent to the very laft?—If you
have rich meadows, which you delight in; and if
the general good requires, that a fort be erected
upon them, or a canal cut thro' them; may you
not be made fenfible that the public has a *fuperior*
right to your property; and that your ground is
not fo *abfolutely* your own, but you may be compelled to part with it for the good of the kingdom?—If you have a fhip laden with goods
brought from the Levant, and you want to fell
them immediately to prevent their being fpoiled;
and if there is fome reafon to fear, that they will
convey the plague; may not a magiftrate, in fpite
of you and a hundred reprefentatives, if you had
a right to chufe fo many, force you to let your
goods fpoil, rather than to endanger the lives of
thoufands?—And, to come to the cafe of the Colonifts, if you and your reprefentative fancied, that
you owe nothing to the fovereign for protecting you
in time paft, and that you can very well protect
yourfelves for the time to come; and if, upon fuch
a fancy, you refufed to contribute to the expence
of the general protection; think you the public
　　　　　　　　　　　　　　　　　would

would be duped by your conceit, and grant you to
live as free from taxes in England, as David did
in Ifrael, when he had flain Goliath? Would not
our governors juftly feize upon a proportion of
your property, whether you and your reprefentative
reafonably confented to it; or whether you abfurdly
raifed the neighbourhood by the patriotic cry of
" Tyranny! robbery! and murder?"

Nor is it only our property, which is not *abfolutely* our own, when we live in civil fociety : For
what I have faid of our goods, may be applied to
our perfons. We are not *abfolutely* our own. Hence
it is, that in all civilized countries, when the fovereign wants foldiers for the protection of the
commonwealth, a militia is raifed; and if the lot
falls upon a pacific farmer, notwithftanding his objections, and the oppofition of his parliamentary
reprefentative, he muft bear arms, either in his
own perfon, or in the perfon of his military reprefentative. And when no fuch reprefentatives can
be procured, the men who are able may be perfonally preffed into the fervice of the commonwealth.
Hence it is that, in an emergency, the fovereign
iffues prefs-warrants to raife failors for manning the
fleet. An hardfhip this, which, great as it is, is
not fo great as the general overthrow of the ftate.

II. Your *firft* error about the abfolutenefs of our
property, naturally leads you into a *fecond* concerning ABJECT SLAVERY, which you confound with
loyal fubjection. Hence you fay, p. 34, &c. " If
" there be any *man*, call him by what name you
" pleafe" [you fhould have faid, agreeably to the
cafe in debate, if there be any *fet of men*, call them
by what name you pleafe, law-givers, magiftrates, or
officers of the legiflative power] " who has" [or have]
" a right to take it [his property] without his con-
" fent expreffed by himfelf or reprefentative, what is
" this but the *quinteffence of flavery?* Wherein does
" the cafe of fuch a man differ from that of the
                                        " moft

" *moſt abject ſlave in the univerſe?* God's lieute-
" nants may, it is true, be very mild, and kind,
" and reaſonable in their demands, and require no
" more of ſuch a man than it is highly juſt he
" ſhould pay :—but what then? If my property be
" at their diſpoſal, not my own,—what becomes
" of my liberty? The man that *robs* me of five
" ſhillings only, commits a *robbery* as much as the
" man that robs me of five pounds. The moſt ab-
" ject ſlave in the univerſe may chance to have a
" very good maſter; but ſtill, if he is *at the diſ-*
" *poſal* of his maſter,—he is equally a ſlave when
" treated well as when treated ill."

The plauſibility of this argument reſts upon
the following miſtakes. (1) You ſtill ſuppoſe, that
inſiſting on moderate taxes as a reaſonable equivalent for protection, is a ſpecies of robbery; whereas
ſuch a demand, by the conſent of all men, except
the patriots of the day, is as reaſonable as the demand of a moderate fee, which a diligent lawyer
has upon his client.—(2) You do not conſider, that
the Coloniſts, being indirectly repreſented in parliament, have as much conſented by their *indirect*
repreſentatives, to pay taxes to the parliament, as
the patriots and you have conſented by your *direct*
repreſentatives to be *additionally* taxed in order to
bring the Colonies to reaſon.—(3) The Latin word
Servus, means not only a *ſervant,* but a *bond-man*
and a *ſlave;* and the Engliſh word, *Servitude,*
means both *ſlavery* and the *ſtate of a ſervant.* But
would it be right in me to avail myſelf of this ana-
logy, to put all the patriotic ſervants in the kingdom out of conceit with their *ſervitude,* and to make
them ſhake off the yoke of dependance, under pretence that ſervitude is *abject ſlavery,* whether a ſervant is treated well or ill?—(4) In Hebrew the word
[*obed*] *ſervant,* means both a *ſlave* and a *ſubject.*
But would you have approved of Abſalom's conduct, if, on this account, he had alienated the
minds of his father's *ſubjects,* and made an injudicious populace believe, that whoſoever fully ſub-
mits

mits himſelf to *good* government, commences an
abject ſlave? Who does not ſee the inconcluſive-
neſs of this argument? An *abject ſlave* is bound
to ſubmit himſelf *reaſonably or unreaſonably* to his
lawleſs Sovereign: A *loyal ſubject* is bound to ſubmit himſelf *reaſonably* to his *lawful* Sovereign:
And therefore, as they are both *bound to ſubmit* or
SUBJECT *themſelves* to their Sovereign, they are
both " *abject ſlaves.*" Such logick, Sir, may convert. heated Americans to your overdoing patriotiſm; but, if I am not miſtaken, it will confirm
judicious Britons in their conſtitutional loyalty.—
(5) You conclude your argument by ſaying' " *A*
" SLAVE *is equally a* SLAVE, *when treated well as*
" *when treated ill;*" and you might have added, *A*
SUBJECT *is equally a* SUBJECT *when treated well as*
when treated ill: but then the pill would not have
been properly guilded; and your own loyalty, as
well as piety, would have taken the alarm at a doctrine, which bears ſo hard upon this goſpel precept,
Let every ſoul BE SUBJECT *to the higher Powers.*

For my part, whatever you may ſay of my "meanneſs," I will be the *ſervant,* the *ſubject,* and if you
pleaſe, Sir, the SLAVE of GOOD *government.* I am
determined to glory in the *ſubjection,* of which you
ſeem to be ſo afraid and aſhamed: And applying to
a *freeman* what the Apoſtle ſays of a *Son,* I do not
ſcruple to aſſert, that a freeman, *ſo long as he* lives
in ſociety, and is a SUBJECT, *differeth nothing from a*
SERVANT or SLAVE who " is well treated;" *but* IS
UNDER *governors* [lawgivers and magiſtrates] *until*
the time appointed of his heavenly *Father* for his removing from earth, and leaving the ſociety of mor-
tals. Gal. iv. 1, 2. To oppoſe this doctrine, is to
overthrow *ſubjection* and *government,* which ſtand or
fall together.

III. A word about the ORIGIN OF POWER. I believe with St. Paul, that *The powers that are, are or-*
dained OF GOD, who is the fountain of all power,
and

and the author of all good government. I date the
divine communication of power, from the paradifi-
acal age ; yea, from the hour in which God faid
to Adam and Eve, *Multiply, and replenifh the earth,
and fubdue it, and* HAVE DOMINION *over—every
living thing.* Gen. i. 28. Here, Sir, is the original grant of Power ? and whofoever wantonly *re-
fifteth the Power* which Providence calls him to obey,
breaks this great political charter of God, which
is fo ftrongly and fo frequently confirmed in the
gofpel.

You reply, p. 74, " The firft man could have
" no power to protect and rule mankind, till there
" were fome for him to rule." But is not this a
miftake ? Might not God endue him with a *protective*, as well as with a *prolific* power, before the
earth began to be replenifhed ? Would you not
wonder at my pofitivenefs, if I infifted, that God
could not give to Adam power to *multiply* and *rule*
his fpecies, becaufe his fpecies was not yet multi-
plied, and governable ; and that our Creator *could
have no creative power*, till creatures rofe into pofitive
exiftence ?

But you add, p. 75, " When Adam became a fa-
" ther, he had as much *power* as *any other father* ;"
And p. 77, you afk, " Does not *every father* receive
" *the fame* divine right of dominion ?" afferting
that, " There is nothing to be inferred from the
" parental authority of Adam, but is *equally* ap-
" plicable to all parents without exception." I reply, that it is contrary to all divinity to fay, that
every parent is endued with all the authority, which
Adam was invefted with, when God faid to him,
SUBDUE *the earth, and* HAVE DOMINION. You are
too judicious a divine, not to fpeak a different language in the pulpit. You know, Sir, that Adam
was invefted with characters which he could not
communicate to *all* his pofterity, and which confequently are not common to all men. A fimile will
poffibly convince you of your miftake. King
George the third, is with refpect to his children,
what

what Adam was with refpect to his pofterity. He
is a *Father*, and a *King*. The *firft* character he
can entail upon all his fons; but the *fecond* he can
entail upon none but the prince of Wales. This
fhews the inconclufivenefs of the argument you draw
from " Eve's motherhood," and " petticoat government." I reverence the queen; and, if fhe
filled the throne as queen Ann did, I would fubmit myfelf to her good government, not becaufe
of Eve's motherhood, but becaufe God faid to *Eve*
[as well as to *Adam*] in her regal capacity, *Have
dominion*; and becaufe he fays in the decalogue,
Honour thy [political] *Mother*, as well as thy political *Father*. Nor fhould I be afhamed to advance
thefe two capital fcriptures in fupport of the Englifh conftitution, if you excited me to dethrone an
Englifh queen, and urged the propriety of the *loi
falique*—a French law this, which, in all cafes, ex-
cludes princeffes from the right of fucceeding to the
crown.

You try to embarrafs the queftion by faying, p.
79, " You muft tell us who is Adam's heir. What
" does it fignify what *power* Adam had, or what
" *power* he left behind him to his" [*governing*]
" fucceffors; unlefs we certainly know who thofe
" fucceffors are." But I reply, that, in every
country, thofe who fhare in the dominion given to
Adam and Eve in their regal capacity, are as much
known as the king and parliament are known in
England, the doge and fenate at Venice, the emperor and diet in Germany, the monarch in France,
and the defpot in Pruffia. Whoever, by the good
providence of God, is endued with the legiflative
and protective power in the country where I refide,
and retains that power by the confent of a majority
of the people, is the *higher power* which I confider as actually *ordained* OF GOD for my protection. To *that* power I will chearfully fubmit, fo
far as it is ufed for good: And to *that* power I will
confcientioufly pay taxes, for the protection which
I enjoy

I enjoy. And fuppofe that power was poffeffed by
an ufurper, I would lament the ufurpation, and
bear my teftimony againft it, till the fame over-
ruling providence which removed Abfalom, John
of Leyden, Ket, the Rump, and Cromwell, took
that ufurper out of the way alfo. But if divine
providence, inftead of removing the ufurper, eftablifhed his power, as it did that of Jeroboam
in the days of Solomon's fon, which I would know
by the general and lafting confent of the people,
I would no longer oppofe that power, but fubmit myfelf to it as religioufly as the chriftians
of the fourth century did to Conftantine the Great,
and as chearfully as the French do to the ancient
family of the *Capets*; tho' *Hugues Capet*, the
firft king of that illuftrious houfe, was only a noble ufurper. Such are, if I miftake not, the loyal
views which the fcripture gives us of the origin of
power; and fuch the marks, by which we may
know the power that divine providence calls us to
obey.

Confider we now what are *your* views of the fame
doctrine. Page 66, you fay, " Every good go-
" vernment is of God. Nor will the perfonal vices
" of our *Governors*, nor any flight error in their
" adminiftaation of government, juftify our refift-
" ing them." Here, Sir, you fpeak as a chriftian and a Briton; and, fo far, I heartily fet my feal
to your politics. But who are our *Governors?*
Are they not the men who are invefted with *governing*, *legiflative*, and *fupreme* power? Now, Sir, according to this juft definition of the word *Governors*, you have thrown down the diftinction between
the governors and *the governed*, and. before you are
aware, you have crowned king *Mob*. I prove my
affertion by your own words. Page 71, you write,
" Perhaps you will fay, The supreme Power in
" every government, muft be lodged fomewhere,
" and this power muft be omnipotent and uncon-
" trolable. I allow it. But the glory of the Britifh
　　　　　　　　" conftitution

" conftitution is, that THE PEOPLE have never
" parted with THIS power, but have MOST RELI-
" GIOUSLY kept it IN THEIR OWN HANDS."
Thus, Sir, according to your doctrine, the su-
PREME and GOVERNING power, belongs not to the
GOVERNORS, but to THE PEOPLE, that is, to THE
GOVERNED. Was ever a more prepofterous doctrine impofed upon injudicious patriots? O Sir,
what you call " *the glory of the Britifh conftitution*,"
would be the *fhame* of the worft government. Nay,
upon this plan, there could be no government at
all. For, fo long as the GOVERNED " *mofi religi-*
" *oufly*" [fhould you not have faid *moft impioufly* and
abfurdly] *keep the* [GOVERNING] *power in their own
hands*, that power is in every body's hands. And
the moment this is the cafe, there is an end of government ; anarchy takes place ; king *Mob* breaks
all the laws with an high hand ; and a tyrannical
populace fiercely trample upon all order, and carry
devaftation wherever they turn their fteps. Thus,
Sir, you have helped me to prove the truth of this
deep propofition of judicious Mr. Baxter, who, after having ftudied chriftian politics near thirty years,
left it upon record, that, " If once legiflation, the
" *chief act of government*, be denied to be any part
" of government at all, and affirmed to belong to
" *the people* as fuch, who are *no governors*, ALL GO-
" VERNMENT WILL THEREBY BE OVERTHROWN,"
—and the grand principle of the fierce, mobbing,
and levelling † Anabaptifts will be " *moft religioufly*"
fet up.

This

† I call *fome* Anabaptifts *fierce and levelling*, to diftinguifh them
from the " *mild and moderate Anabaptifts*," whom I have mentioned *Vind.* p. 46, where I commend the *candor* of Bifhop Burnet
for making a juft diftinction between thefe two forts of Anabaptifts; and for obferving, that " *they were not all of the fame temper.*" This, one would think, fhould have hindered our brethren who contend for anabaptifm, to think that I reflect on *all*

This doctrine of yours, Sir, brings to my remembrance an anecdote, to which a loyal and pious Anabaptist undesignedly helped me some weeks ago. In order to convince me that what Mr. Baxter says of the high republican spirit of the Anabaptists and Independents is not true, he sent me the IVth volume of *Blennerhaffet's History of England,*
which

---

the people of their denomination, for the political errors of *some.* Had I done this, I would publicly afk their pardon ; being persuaded that nothing can be more cruel, than to involve the innocent in undeserved guilt. Left this construction should be put upon my quotations respecting the levelling Anabaptists, I inserted in the second edition of my Vindication, p. 46, a note where I say, that ' *some Anabaptists are very good people,* that *most of them mean* ' *well,* and that *I hope this is the case with my opponent.*" And I gladly embrace this third opportunity of testifying more fully my brotherly love to that respectable body of dissenters ; not doubting but there are numbers of truly pious and loyal Anabaptists both in Germany, England, and America. However, p. 84, my opponent says, " *Your telling the world that I am, &c. an Anabap-* " *tist,* &c. *is a display of illiberality, meanness, and impertinence.*" But where did I tell the world, in the first edition of my book, that Mr. Evans is an Anabaptist ? And if in a note inserted in the *second* edition [which, by the bye, was not published when Mr. E. advanced this charge] I *insinuate* that he is one of the Anabaptists who " *are very good people and mean well;*" I appeal to the unprejudiced, if this infinuation, is not a display of *candor* and *brotherly love,* rather than of " *illiberallity, meanness, and impertinence?*" I grant that I have inforced *Calvin's* doctrine of taxation upon my opponent, by reminding him, that, as " *he is a Calvinist,*" he cannot well avoid paying some regard to that excellent doctrine of *Calvin.* But wherein consists the *impertinence* of such an argument ? Are controvertists the only men, who cannot use an argument *ad hominem?* And has not Mr. E. as much reason to charge me with " *meanness,*" because I have addressed him as a *Briton* and a *Christian,* and have pressed him, as such, with appeals to *constitutional* conceffions, and his *Christian* profession ? Some men will say what they please against their governors. Their most groundless charges must pass for patriotism, and a spirited defence of our liberties ; but if you drop a felf-evident truth that embarraffes them a little, you are guilty of " *Helvetic* rudeness, illiberallity, meanness, and impertinence." I appeal from this patriotic freedom and partiality, to English candor, and British politeness.

which contains an account of the proceedings of
the mangled tyrannical parliament known by the
name of *the Rump*. This author informs us,
p. 1541, that juſt before king Charles I. was
beheaded, " The Commons voted, that *the people*,
" under God, are *the original* of all juſt power ;
" and that the Commons of England being cho-
" ſen by the people, had the *ſupreme* authority of
" this nation ; and what *they* enacted ſhould be
" law, without the king or lords' concurrence.
" This ſquared exactly with the Independents,
" who were for turning the monarchy into a re-
" public." Now if the *Anabaptiſts* were at leaſt
as zealous republicans as the *Independents*, I leave
you to judge, Sir, if my neighbour's book was a
better proof of Baxter's miſtake than your own ;
and if it is not evident from this quotation, that
when you teach the world, that *the people muſt re-
ligiouſly keep the ſupreme power* [i. e. the power of
their governors] *in their own hands*, as their indubitable right, you plow with the wild, miſchievous
heifer of Cromwell and the rump.

IV. A word concerning the PROPER CAUSE
of the war with America.

Page 51, you ſay, " Should it be made to ap-
" pear, that the Britiſh parliament have authority
" from ſcripture to tax their unrepreſented bre-
" thren in America, and to *cut their throats*, burn
" their towns, and ſpread univerſal devaſtation
" amongſt them, becauſe they do not chuſe to
" ſubmit to ſuch taxation : it would furniſh a
" ſtronger objection, &c. againſt the divine origi-
" nal of the ſacred code, than has ever yet been
" produced." You inſinuate by theſe words, that
the PROPER and IMMEDIATE cauſe of *cutting
throats* in America, is the demand which the king
and parliament make of taxes ? But are you not

C   miſtaken.

miſtaken, Sir? And does not your miſtake make you throw an undeſerved odium upon the ſovereign? For my part I conceive, that the *immediate* occaſion of the bloodſhed which we lament, is not ſo much the parliamentary demand of taxes, as a chain of cauſes, which chiefly contains the following links: (1) The heat of ſome Boſtonian patriots, who, with felonious audacity, boarded our ſhips, ſeized upon the property of our merchants, and wantonly threw it into the ſea. If the patriots would not buy tea ſubjected to a tax, could they not keep their own money? Was it right in them to undo our innocent traders by deſtroying their goods?—(2) The demand which the government made of reſtitution, or ſatisfaction, for that act of glaring injuſtice: a *juſt* demand this, which the ſovereign could not avoid making without being guilty of injuſtice; it being evident, that it would be unjuſt in the legiſlative power, to receive taxes of our merchants for the protection of their property, and then to look on unconcerned, when that property is feloniouſly deſtroyed.—(3) The obſtinacy with which the mobbing patriots, and their abettors, refuſed to make ſatisfaction to our injured merchants.—(4) The prudence with which the parliament farther interpoſed, by paſſing the bill for ſhutting up the port of Boſton, that by this unbloody and mild method, the Boſtonians might gently be brought to make reſtitution.—And laſtly, the flame of revolt, which on this occaſion rapidly ſpread thro' Britiſh America.

Had the Algerines inſulted the Britiſh flag, and injured Britiſh ſubjects, as the mobbing Boſtonians have done; the government would not have ſhewn them the ſame lenity. A fleet would immediately have ſailed for the inhoſpitable coaſt; and the admiral would have ſent a card to the legiſlature of Algiers: "I am come to demand ſatisfaction for the injury done to Britiſh ſubjects. Send me, by to-morrow, 30,000 l. being the value of the goods which

which you, or the men whom you screen, have feloniously taken from our merchants; or I will do them and my country justice." Instead of using this peremptory method, as Admiral Blake would have done; our admiral quietly stationed his ships before Boston, and General Gage, far from " cutting throats," amicably quartered his forces in or about that city; patiently waiting till remorse of conscience, a sense of equity, a spark of loyalty, or some fear of the power, wrought upon the patriots, so called, and inclined them to do an act of justice, which Mahometans would hardly have refused to do. But all in vain. The mobbing patriots and their ringleaders, hardened by this lenity, avail themselves of the kind delay. While humanity and brotherly love suspend the stroke of justice, enthusiastic demagogues found a false alarm, and engage the misinformed Colonists to countenance their obstinacy. In short, the Americans, seduced by misrepresentations, take up arms against Great Britain: and the forces sent by the sovereign, instead of obtaining the satisfaction they demand, are obliged to provide for their own safety by attempting to seize some of the artillery, and ammunition, brought from all quarters to destroy them. Hence the engagement at *Lexington*, and the fight at *Bunker's Hill*, where the forces raised by the congress pressed those of the sovereign by an audacious blockade.

Should you object, that the Colonists once offered to make restitution, on condition that they should never be taxed by the power that protected them : I reply, that by such an offer they only added injustice and revolt to felony. Suppose the Scotch plundered an English ship, and the sovereign insisted on speedy restitution; do you think they would deserve the name of *patriots*, if they said : We will pay for the goods we have destroyed, on condition that you shall exempt us from paying the window-tax for ever. Or, in other

terms,

terms, We will be juſt to ſome of our fellow-ſub-
jects, if you will give us leave to wrong all our
fellow ſubjects, to ſhake off your authority, and
to break Chriſt's capital commandment, *Render to
all their* DUES, eſpecially taxes *to Cæſar.*

If this is a true ſtate of the caſe, are you not
partial, Sir, when you repreſent the parliament as
" *cutting the throats*" of the Coloniſts, becauſe the
Coloniſts will not be taxed by the parliament? Is
it not rather the Coloniſts, who want to *cut the
throats* of our ſoldiers, becauſe the king and parliament juſtly inſiſt on proper ſatisfaction for the
injury done to Britiſh merchants by the petty ty-
rants of Boſton?

An illuſtration will make you ſtill more ſenſible
of your miſtake. Suppoſe I harbour a parcel of
houſe-breakers, or ſhip-breakers, who have ſtolen
or deſtroyed your goods; and ſuppoſe you obtain
a legal warrant, and come attended with a number of armed conſtables to recover your property,
or apprehend the felons; if I raiſe a mob to hinder the conſtables from doing their office, and if
ſome *throats are cut* in the endeavour which the
conſtables make not to fall into the hands of the
armed mob which ſurrounds them; is the guilt of
cutting throats, chargeable upon *you,* who act *according to law,* and in a *juſt* cauſe? Is it not rather chargeable upon *me,* who wantonly oppoſe
the legiſlative power, and can ſay nothing in defence of myſelf and my mob, but that the felons
I protect are not felons, but ſpirited patriots; or
that I ſhall pay you for damages, if you will promiſe
to ſuffer yourſelf to be wronged of more money
than the wrong you have ſuſtained amounts to!

Suppoſe that the doctrine of taxation, which is
the *remote* cauſe of our diviſions, admits of ſome
objections, as the plaineſt doctrines always do;
[for the brighteſt clouds have their obſcure ſide,
and the moſt ſhining diamonds caſt a faint ſhade;]
yet the *immediate* cauſe of the American war, the
refuſing

refuſing to make reſtitution for goods feloniouſly deſtroyed, has no ſhadow of difficulty. Whoever is *honeſt* enough, to diſapprove the malicious deſtruction of an innocent man's property;—whoever is *conſcientious* enough, to praiſe the ſteadineſs of a government, which ſtands by oppreſſed ſubjects whom it is bound to protect;—and whoever is ſo far a *lover of order*, as to blame a wanton oppoſition to the ſovereign, when he diſcharges his duty: muſt confeſs, that the guilt of " cutting throats" in America, is *properly* cauſed by the obſtinate injuſtice of the American patriots; and not by the moderate taxes laid by the Britiſh legiſlature. To aſſert the contrary is almoſt as great a miſtake in politicks, as it is in divinity to hint, that the miſeries conſequent upon man's fall, were not *properly* cauſed by the tempter's artful miſrepreſentations, and by Adam's wilful rebellion; but by God's reaſonable demand of a little proof of Adam's loyalty.

And now, Sir, if I have duly confirmed my proofs, that the doctrine of taxation which you oppoſe, is juſt in every point of view;—if I have ſhewn that you confound loyal ſubjection with *abject ſlavery*;—if I have demonſtrated, that your notions concerning the *ſupreme power* of the people, are ſubverſive of all government;—and if I have made appear, that you do not fix the charge of wantonly " *cutting throats*" upon thoſe who are *properly* guilty of that atrocious crime; may I not call upon your rational and moral feelings to decide, if I have not vindicated my Vindication? And are you not as precipitate, when you pronounce me " one of the moſt unmeaning and unfair diſputants that ever took up the polemical gauntlet," as when you inſinuate that the Britiſh legiſlature " *commits robbery*," becauſe it lays a moderate tax upon thoſe who have long baſked in the beams of its protection, and have acquired immenſe wealth under the guardian ſhadow of its flags and ſtandards?

Hoping

Hoping that no controverſial heat will make us forget that we are fellow-creatures, fellow-ſub-jects, fellow-proteſtants, and fellow-labourers in the goſpel of truth and love; I aſk a part in your eſteem, equal to that which [notwithſtanding your heats and miſtakes] you have in the cordial reſpect of,

Rev. Sir,

Your affectionate brother

and obedient ſervant,

J. F.

LETTER III.

Rev. Sir,

IF I have anſwered *you* in the preceding letters, I may look your ſecond in the face : I mean the ingenious Dr. *Price*, whom you call to your help in your notes, and whoſe arguments you introduce by this high encomium : ' Dr. *Price*'s ' moſt excellent pamphlet juſt publiſhed, carries con- ' viction into every page, and breathes that noble ' ſpirit of *liberty*, for which the author ſo ab.y ' pleads.'

Page 46, your firſt quotation from him runs thus : " In the 6th of George II. an act paſſed " for impoſing certain duties on all foreign ſpi- " rits—and ſugars imported into the plantations. " In this act the duties impoſed are ſaid to be gi- " ven and granted by the parliament to the king, " &c. and a ſmall direct revenue was drawn by it " from them."—The Doctor intimates ſoon after, that " this revenue-act was at worſt only the ex- " erciſe of a power, which then they [the Colo- " niſts] ſeem not to have thought much of con- " teſting ; I mean the power of taxing them EX- " TERNALLY." — I thank Dr. Price and you, Sir, for thus granting that the Coloniſts were tax- ed *before* the preſent parliament and the preſent reign. This ſhews that the odium caſt upon the *preſent* government, ſprings more from prejudice than from reaſon. If George II. his whig-miniſ- try, and his approved parliament, raiſed a " direct

C 4   revenue"

revenue" by taxing the Colonies, why do the American patriots infinuate that George III. the prefent miniftry, and the prefent parliament are robbers, becaufe they raife a *direct revenue* by taxing the Colonifts? And how ftrangely does Dr. Price forget himfelf, where he fays; " How great " would be *our happinefs* could we now *recall former* " *times,* and *return to the policy of the laft reigns?*" What have our lawgivers done after all? Truly they have *recalled former times,* and *returned to the policy of the laft reigns;* and yet Dr. P. inftead of being thankful for *our happinefs,* frightens the public with moft dreadful hints about the infatuation of our governors, and the danger of " a general wreck;" juft as if his grand bufinefs was to fpirit up the Colonifts, and to deject his own countrymen.

The Dr. it is true, tries to obviate this difficulty by making a diftinction between external and internal taxes; infinuating that in the late reign the Colonifts were taxed EXTERNALLY, whereas in the prefent reign they have been taxed INTERNALLY. But if this diftinction is frivolous, will it reflect any praife on your patriotifm? And that it is fuch, I prove by the following argument: A diftinction about taxation, which has no foundation in *reafon, fcripture,* or the *conftitution,* is frivolous: But Dr. Price's diftinction has no foundation in reafon, fcripture, or the conftitution: And therefore it is frivolous in the prefent controverfy. Should you conteft the fecond propofition of this fyllogifm, I afk: By what dictates of *reafon* does it appear, that, if taxes are *due* from fubjects to their fovereign, they may not be levied *internally,* by rates upon the goods we already poffefs, as well as *externally,* by duties upon goods imported, which purchafe has not yet made our own? Where does St. Paul charge chriftians to pay taxes, if they are *externally* taxed; and to fly to arms, if they are taxed *internally?* Did not Chrift fpeak of *internal* taxes, when he commanded the

the Jews to *render Cæfar* what was his? And is
there any law, either of God or of the realm, which
allows the legiflative power to tax the fubjects of
Great Britain *externally*, and precludes it from taxing them *internally?*

The Doctor's diftinction is not only unfcriptural
and unconftitutional, but *unreafonable*; in as much
as it would, in a great degree, enable fubjects to·
avoid paying taxes at all. Suppofe, for example,
we could be taxed only EXTERNALLY, by means of
duties laid upon *imported* goods, fuch as tea, coffee,
foreign wines, and rum; might we not, if I may
fo fpeak, *ftarve the government* by drinking only
fage or balm-tea, ale, made-wines, and fpirits dif-
tilled from our own wheat?—The Doctor's diftinction is not only unreafonable, but *unjuft.* Why
fhould the Colonies enjoy greater privileges than
the mother-country? Why fhould Britons be taxed *externally* and *internally*, whether they have votes
or not, and the Americans ONLY *externally*; when
both have· their property *internally* and *externally*
guarded by the protective power? If I owed my
lawyer reafonable fees amounting to ten pounds;
what would you think of my honefty, if I faid to·
him, Sir, I give you leave to pay yourfelf by demanding a fhilling from me, every time I drink a
glafs of claret or a difh of chocolate: but I declare
to you, that, except in fuch cafes, I will take you·
for a robber, if you lay claim to any part of my
property?—The Doctor's diftinction is not only
unjuft in the prefent cafe, but it might prove *deftructive* to the commonwealth. It is granted on all
fides, that taxes and money are the finews of the
government. If *external* taxes did not bring in
money enough to difcharge the neceffary expences
of the ftate; and if the fovereign could not lay *internal* taxes to fupply that deficiency, what would
become of the kingdom? Muft it not fall a wanton facrifice to Dr. Price's political refinements?
I hope, Sir, that if you weigh thefe obfervations,.

you

you will own that his book, ingenious as it is,
far from " carrying conviction in every page,"
carries frivolousness, and mischievous absurdity
in the very first quotation, which you produce
from him.   And we may well suppose, you did not
pick out his weakest argument, to support the prais-
es which you bestow on his " most excellent pamphlet."

But let us hear him out. You continue, p. 47,
to quote him thus. " The *stamp-act* was passed.
" This being an attempt to tax them *internally*;
" and a direct attack on their property, by a power
" which would not suffer itself to be questioned;
" which eased *itself* by loading them; and to which
" it was impossible to fix any bounds; they were
" thrown at once, from one end of the continent
" to the other, into resistance and rage." This
sounds well to the ear; but judicious patriots, who
expect to find the kernel of truth under the specious
shell of fine words, may be a little disappointed.
Permit me, Sir, to break the shell, and to see if
the kernel is found.

(1) *An attempt to tax* subjects INTERNALLY is a
direct attack on their property! And what if it is?
When reasonable taxes are *due*, may they not be *directly* demanded? And that they are *due*, do you
not grant p. 27, where you so much resent my supposing, that you deny " *the* NECESSITY *of subjects
paying taxes*," whether they be external or internal?
—(2) The legislative *power* of Great Britain *would
not suffer itself to be questioned!* The Doctor should
have said, that it *would not suffer itself* to be deprived
of it's right of demanding reasonable taxes, for ex-
pensive protection; an incontestible right this, which,
you allow, none deny but " political Quixotes."—
(3) But this *power eases* ITSELF *by loading* THEM!
And what if it does? Is the sovereign to bear all
the national expence, without being *eased* by his
subjects? Or are *some* of the subjects to bear all the
burden, without being *eased* by others who are able
to

to help them? Where is either the equity or rea-
fonableneſs of this objection?—(4) But it is *impoſſible to fix any bounds to this power!* I have already
ſhewn, that nothing can be eaſier than to fix proper
bounds to the power of taxing the Colonies. The
parliament can enact, that the Coloniſts ſhall be taxed as the Britons are; making the Coloniſts a proper
allowance for the ſuperior commercial privileges of
the mother-country. Suppoſing, for inſtance, that
the privileges of Britiſh ſubjects are four times greater than the privileges of American ſubjects, the taxes of the American ſubjects might be four times lighter than ours. Thus, when we pay four ſhillings in
the pound, they might pay only one ſhilling: and
when four articles of equal importance are taxed in
England, only one might be taxed in America. It
is therefore exceſſively wrong in Dr. Price to aſſert,
that it is *impoſſible to fix any bounds to the power* of
parliamentary taxation. And none but heated patriots will praiſe him for encreaſing, by ſuch a ground-
leſs aſſertion, the abſurd " *rage into which the Colo-*
" *niſts*" have " *thrown*" themſelves "*from one end*
" *of the continent to the other.*"

Page 48, You take up again ' Dr. Price's truly
' valuable tract, and enrich' your ' piece with a
' note from this capital writer upon the ſubject. In
' reference to the American charters, he ſpeaks with
' true dignity as follows:—" The queſtion with all
" liberal enquirers ought to be, not what juriſdic-
" tion over them [the colonies] precedents, ſta-
" tutes, and charters give, but what reaſon and equi-
" ty, and the rights of humanity give." Sir, this
is the very firſt teſt, to which I have brought your
" American patriotiſm." The Doctor inſinuates indeed, that the power, which taxes the Americans,
will not ſuffer it's rights to be *queſtioned.* But this
is a miſtake. The legiſlature of Great Britain is
too equitable, not to give up the right of reaſonably
taxing the Coloniſts, whom they have ſo long protected; if you, Sir, Dr. Price, or the Congreſs, can

prove that *reafon, equity*, and *the rights of humanity*
are againſt ſuch taxation. Have you not yourſelf
granted the *propriety and neceſſity of* SUBJECTS *paying*
proportionable *taxes* for the good of the whole empire? Is it *reaſonable* or *equitable*, that Great Britain ſhould bear all the burden of the navy, which
protects the Colonies and their trade? Is it contrary to " *the rights of humanity*" to demand a penny for
a penny-loaf, or, which comes to the ſame thing,
to demand reaſonable taxes for royal protection? Or
do parent-ſtates violate " *the rights of humanity*" in
demanding ſome aſſiſtance from the growing ſtates,
to which they have given birth, when thoſe ſtates
are well able to bear the eaſy burden? As ſoon will
Dr. Price perſuade me, that it is contrary to " *the
rights of humanity*" in twelve lubberly young fellows,
who have always enjoyed the benefit of their father's
houſe, and who can get more money than their father, to give him ſomething towards the payment
of the window-tax, when he is burdened with debts,
and wants ſome aſſiſtance to pay that tax.

    Page 49, You continue to quote the Doctor thus :
" Did they not ſettle under the faith of charters,
" which promiſed them the enjoyment of all the
" rights of *Engliſhmen* ?" Granted. But did theſe
charters promiſe them rights *ſuperior* to thoſe of Engliſhmen? Is it not evident, that if the Coloniſts enjoy
the right of being protected by the legiſlative power
of Great Britain, without paying taxes to that power,
they enjoy a right *ſuperior* to that of Engliſhmen,
who are bound to pay taxes for Britiſh protection?

    The Doctor goes on. " Theſe charters allowed
" them to tax themſelves, and to be governed by
" legiſlatures of their own, ſimilar to ours."
Granted in one ſenſe : namely in the ſame ſenſe, in
which charters have been granted to corporations.
Corporate bodies are allowed to tax themſelves in a
ſubordinate manner, and to be governed by legiſlatures of their own, ſimilar to that of Great Britain.
Thus the city of London is governed by a Lord
Mayor, who repreſents the King; by a court of
aldermen,

aldermen, which reprefents the high court of parliament; and by a body of livery-men and freemen, which anfwers to the body of voting burgeffes
and freeholders in Great Britain. And I fuppofe
all together can raife money for the fupport of the
corporation, by means of fome peculiar rates, or
fubordinate taxes. Now if the citizens of London
rofe againft parliamentary taxation, under pretence
that they are, and always have been taxed by their
own magiftrates; they would fhew themfelves as
unjuft as the Colonifts, and as good logicians as Dr.
Price. What have *fubordinate* taxes for the maintenance of lamp-lighters, watchmen, and trained
bands, to do with the *primary* taxes, by which the
army and the navy are fupported? When rafh patriots avail themfelves of the payment of the former taxes, to refufe paying the latter : do they
fhew more wifdom and equity than I fhould do, if I
quarrelled with my phyfician for demanding of
me ten guineas for ten vifits, and difmiffed him
with the following fpeech: Sir, I claim all the
rights of Englifhmen, nor will I be duped by you
I do not deny paying fees, but I will not pay any
to *you*. I will difcharge my *apothecary's* bill; but
as for *your* demands, they are contrary to " *reafon,*
" *equity, and the rights of humanity.*" American
patriots might give me thanks, and compliment me
with the freedom of London in a golden box, for
fuch a fpirited oppofition to tyranny and robbery ;
but I am of opinion, that Britifh patriots would hardly think me worthy of the freedom of Old Sarum in
a wooden *box*: And if the phyfician was " *thrown*
" *into rage*" by my provoking injuftice, he might
poffibly think that I deferved a very different *box,*
from that which Dr. Price has been lately prefented
with.

But the Doctor has an anfwer ready. Speaking
of the Colonifts he fays. " They are taxed to fup-
" port their own governments :—Muft they main-
" tain *two* governments? Muft they fubmit to be
" *triple* taxed?" To fhew the frivoloufnefs of this
                                                argument,

argument, I need only farther apply it to my phyfician's cafe thus: Sir, you demand fees of me for your
attendance, but I have already feed my apothecary :
Muft I maintain *two* of you? Muft I fubmit to be
triple taxed? What ! muft I pay my furgeon too!
You unreafonable men, will you all agree to enflave
me ? You pack of r——s, will you *leave me nothing*
that I can call my own ?

Whilft you are ftruck with the fallacy of this patriotic argument, I proceed to fome obfervations
upon Dr. Price's doctrine, with refpect to the CHAR-
TERS of the Colonies. To fuppofe, that their charters exempt them from paying taxes to the Britifh
government for ever, is not only contrary to the
exprefs terms of the charter of Penfylvania ; but
alfo to all probability. What ruling power would.
be fo unwife as to fuffer the emigration of fubjects,
out of a country which is not overftocked with in-
habitants, into one where that power has claims
and poffeffions, unlefs it was affured of retaining
the right of *fupremacy* over thofe emigrated fubjects ?
Is it reafonable to think, that a power would thus
weaken itfelf? And is it not the right of *fupreme*
taxation infeparably connected with the right of *fu-*
preme government ?

Again : When one of our kings granted a charter to the Colonifts, did he not grant it as being the
head of the legiflative *power* of Great Britain :——
a *power* this, whofe fhips had taken poffeffion of
North America? Was it not as the reprefentative
of *all* this power, that he figned the charter ? Suppofe the Lord Mayor of London, as political head
of that city, had granted me leave to build a houfe
upon fome wafte ground belonging to the city : and
fuppofe he had helped me to build it with fome ma-
terials, the property of the city, and had from time
to time preferved it from being robbed and burned,
by fending me watchmen, fire-men, and fire-
engines from the city ; would it be right in me to
fay, I acknowledge myfelf indebted to the Lord
Mayor, as a *Lord*; but as for his London-mayoralty,

alty, and the council of aldermen, I bid them de-
fiance, and deny my being under the leaft obligation of fubmitting myfelf to them. In fhort, I am
willing that the Mayor of London fhould be my
governor; but if the body of the corporation claims
authority over me, and demands of me, who am
neither one of the livery nor a freeman, city rates to
pay the watchmen or buy new fire-engines, I will
fhew both them and the Lord Mayor, that I am a *patriot*, and that I can defend my property and protect
my perfon.—Could you help fmiling at the abfurdity of fuch a fpeech? And think you, Dr. Price
himfelf could prove, that the diftinction which the
Colonifts make between the *king* and the *parliament*,
—between the *head* and the *body* of the Britifh legiflature, is not as trifling and ungenerous, as the
diftinction I make between the *Lordfhip of the Mayor
of London*, and the *London-mayoralty*; or between
the *head*, and the *body* of that refpectable corporation?

To return : After faying that the arguments drawn
from the charters *for* the Colonies appear to him
" greatly to outweigh the arguments *againft* them,"
Dr. Price fpeaks thus : " But I lay no ftrefs on
" charters. They [the Colonies] derive their
" rights from a higher fource. It is inconfiftent
" with common fenfe to imagine, that any people
" would ever think of fettling in a diftant country,
" on any fuch condition, as that the people from
" whom they withdrew, fhould for ever be mafters.
" of their property, and have power to fubject them
" to any modes of government they pleafed."—The
flaw of this argument confifts in imputing to Great-
Britain, falfe claims, which never entered into the
minds of our legiflators. When did the parliament
fay, they would " *for ever be mafters of the property of
the Colonifts*," any otherwife than they are mafters of
the property of Englifhmen ?—If the king and parliament claim the right of " making ftatutes of fufficient force to bind the colonies in *all cafes whatfoever*,"

does

does not candor dictate, that they only mean all cafes
wherein they have power to bind Englifhmen ?—
And is not Dr. Franklin too warm, when, availing
himfelf of the laconic manner in which this reafonable claim is expreffed, he renders the legiflative
power odious, by infinuating that it pretends to the
authority of " *compelling* the Colonifts, if it pleafes,
" to worfhip the devil ?—Once more : When did
the Britifh legiflature claim the right of "*fubjecting*
" the Americans *to any modes of government they*
" *pleafe*," whether thefe modes be ever fo foolifh or
tyrannical ? Is it not wrong in Dr. Price and Dr.
Franklin, to fix upon our doctrine invidious confequences, which have not the leaft connexion with
our principles ? What character could I not blaft,
and whom could I not reprefent as a rapacious tyrant,
if I intimated, that, whenever a mafter claims the
authority of *reafonably* commanding his fervants in all
things, he affumes the authority of making them
" worfhip the devil if he pleafes ;" and that, whenever the Lord of a manor infifts on his chiefrie, a
lawyer on his fees, a minifter on his tithes, and a
Sovereign on reafonable taxes ; they pretend to be
" *for ever mafters of the property*' of their vaffals, te-
nants, clients, flocks, and fubjects ; fo that the *abject flaves can call nothing which they have their own ?*
Can we lament too much the miftake of divines,
who, by fuch ungenerous infinuations, inflame the
heated patriots, and pour contempt on their rightful
governors.

Page 49, You continue to quote Dr. Price thus :
" Had there been exprefs ftipulations to this pur-
" pofe in all the charters of the Colonies, they
" would, in my opinion, be no more bound by
" them, than if it had been ftipulated with them,
" that they fhould go naked, or expofe themfelves
" to the incurfions of wolves and tygers." The
Doctor is highly worthy to be your fecond, Sir.
We have feen how you confound the right, which
the protecting power has to reafonable taxes, with
the right which an highwayman has to a traveller's
money :

money : and we fee here that Dr. Price abfurdly compares a fcriptural demand of moderate taxes, with an immodeft command of going naked ; and with a tyrannical edict of encountering " wolves and tygers." If fuch method of arguing is confiftent either with found logic or chriftian candor, I confent that the Doctor's gold-box be fet with rubies and diamonds.

The Doctor's argument is not only founded on an abfurd comparifon ; but it can alfo be retorted in this manner : " *I lay no ftrefs on charters :*" The king and parliament " *derive their rights*" of taxing their American fubjects " *from an higher fource.*" " *Had there been exprefs ftipulations in all the Charters*, that the Colonies fhould ever be protected by Great-Britain, without paying proportionable taxes as other fubjects, it may be queried if the king and parliament would he any *more bound by* fuch ftipulations, than they would be bound by a charter of the late king. fuppofing he had granted to all the Scotchmen and Yorkfhiremen who have no vote, the privilege of paying no taxes to the government for ever. Might not fuch a charter be repealed on account of its unjuft partiality ? Should not the taxes be laid as proportionably as it is poffible upon all the fubjects ? Can the king abfolutely give up the rights of one part of his fubjects to the other, any more than he can juftly fay, that when the parliament lays a tax of 4s. in the pound, Middlefex fhall pay nothing for ever, becaufe the trade of London brings in an immenfe revenue to the government ? If thefe queries recommend themfelves to your reafon, Sir ; is it not evident that Dr. Price's argument can be properly retorted, and that he is equally miftaken, whether he appeals to " charters," or to " an higher fource ?"

Pafs we on to his doctrine concerning the ORIGIN OF POWER. P. 69, You introduce him as fpeaking thus : " I am fenfible, that all I have been " faying would be very abfurd, were the opinions " juft, which fome have maintained concerning
" the

" the origin of government. According to these
" opinions, government is not *the creature of the*
" *people* or the result of a convention between
" them and their rulers: But there are certain men
" who possess in themselves, independently on the
" will of the people, a right of governing them,
" which they derive from the Deity." From this
quotation it is evident, that, according to Dr. Price's
principles and your own, "*Government is the creature*
" *of the people.*" In full opposition to this doctrine
I assert that *Government is the creature of . God.* It is
as absurd to say, that government is the creature of
the people, as to maintain, that *religion* and *marriage*
are the creatures of the people. All that I can reasonably grant the Doctor is, that as adultery and for-
nication, superstition and idolatry are the creatures
of immoral and irreligious men; so *bad* government, which includes *confusion* and *tyranny*, is the
creature of wicked men.

Government is not less necessary in the moral
world, than the subordinate motion of the planets
in the natural. As God appointed the *greater*
luminaries to rule the day and the night; so he appointed the higher powers to rule the less. When
he manifested himself to rationals by his works or
his word, and impressed their minds with a sense
of their high obligations to him, he instituted RE-
LIGION. When he said, *I will make man an help*
meet for him, and joined Adam and Eve together in
their *human* capacity; bidding them *increase* and
multiply, he instituted MARRIAGE. And when he
said to them, in their *regal* capacity, *Have dominion*;
he delegated governing power, and instituted GO-
VERNMENT on earth; or, to speak more properly,
he caused that celestial plant to take root in paradise; whence, with divers degrees of degeneracy,
it has overspread the civilized parts of the earth.
If this is the case, is not Dr. Price under a capital
mistake, when he makes government " the creature
" of the people?" And does he not flatly contradict St. James, who says, *Do not err: Every good*
gift

gift [and confequently GOVERNMENT, one of the beft public gifts] *is from above, and cometh down from the Father of lights* ?

You will probably endeavour to render this doctrine odious by infinuating, that it makes the people altogether paffive in matter of *government, religion,* and *marriage.* Nay, Dr. Price does it already where he fays, that, according to the fcheme he oppofes, fome men poffefs a right of governing " independently on the will of the people." This affertion is true in one fenfe, and falfe in another. It is true that the higher powers muft govern the lefs, and that Sovereigns have a right of ruling their fubjects for good, " *independently on the will* " *of the people.*" That is, fuppofing the people wantonly dethroned their Sovereigns, to fet up anarchy on the ruins of every legiflature; it is true that fuch fovereigns fhould ftill have a *right* to rule fuch unruly fubjects; juft as a captain, againft whom his foldiers wantonly rife, has ftill a *right* to command them, *whether they will be commanded or not.* If this were not true, rebellion and treafon were no fin at all; the heinoufnefs of thofe crimes confifting in a wanton refifting of a power, which poffeffes a right of governing us, *whether we will be governed or not.* But if Dr. Price intimates, that our doctrine fuppofes *the will of the people* has abfolutely no fhare in our doctrine of government, he greatly miftakes : For we think that the will of a majority of the *people* is as indifpenfably neceffary to the fupport of *civil* government in the ftate, as the will of a majority of the *foldiers* is neceffary to the fupport of *military* government in the army. Neverthelefs the confent of the people to be governed by their Sovereign, and of the foldiers to be commanded by their general, is not the ground or origin of the Sovereign's and general's authority. It is only [caufa fine qua non] a requifite, without which, Sovereigns and generals cannot exercife their authority.

Some

Some illuftrations may help you to underftand
this nice point of doctrine. Men are bound to
pay God a *reafonable* fervice, whether they will
or not. A wife is bound to obey her hufband in
all reafonable things, whether willingly or un-
willingly. And fubjects are bound to obey their
fovereign in all reafonable and lawful things, however averfe they may be to it. Nor is it lefs abfurd to make a lawful fovereign's claim to the obedience of his fubjects, depend upon *their will*;
than to make the right which a hufband has of
ruling his wife, depend upon *her caprice*; or the
right which God has to our adoration, turn upon
our confent. Neverthelefs if wives will abfolutely
refufe to fubmit to their hufbands, finners to their
God, and fubjects to their king, they can fhake
off the yoke of fubjection, and affect domeftic, religious, and civil independence. But then the pur-
pofes of marriage, religion and government are de-
feated; and a threefold rebellion takes place.

It will be proper here to trace back to its fource
the error about liberty, which Dr. Price has adopted
from *Rouffeau*, the great Geneva patriot: A fatal
error this, by which that fanciful politician has
kindled the flame of difcord in his own country,
This error confifts in inferring, that, becaufe a favage, who lives alone in a wood, is his own governor, and can legiflate for himfelf; a man, who lives
in civil fociety can do the fame. But is not this as
abfurd as to fuppofe, that becaufe a man who is not
lifted, and of courfe is under no military government, can go backward or forward when he pleafes:
therefore a foldier in the field of battle has a right
to legiflate for himfelf, and advance or retire juft
when he thinks proper?

I grant that if a number of favages, living like
wild beafts without *religion, marriage*, and *government*, could be prevailed on to enter upon a religious, conjugal and civil life; among all the religi-
ons, women, and governments which they could
chufe, they might undoubtedly *chufe* thofe which
they

they thought beſt. This, after a cloſe enquiry, would be both their right and their duty. And ſuppoſe they had miſtaken idolatry for religion, an inceſtous union for marriage, and tyranny for government; they would be bound to alter their plan, becauſe ſuch capital miſtakes are deſtructive of the ſalutary ends propoſed in *religion, marriage,* and *government.* Again: When they had agreed to embrace a religious, conjugal, and civil life; they might agree to *worſhip* God ſtanding or kneeling, in open air or in church, in hymns or in prayers, &c. They might agree to *marry* before two witneſſes, or two hundred, and to do it by giving and receiving a ring, or only by joining hands. And they might embrace a monarchical, ariſtocratical, or democratical government; or they might, as the Engliſh have done, combine thoſe three ſorts of governments, and ſubmit at once to a king, an houſe of lords, and an houſe of commons. But if they had once eſpouſed a true religion, lawful wives, and a lawful government; they would ſin againſt God, their neighbour, and their own ſouls; —they would be guilty of impiety, adultery, and rebellion; if they wantonly changed their religion, their wives, and their ſovereign.

The reaſon is evident. Men who never had any religion, wife, or ſovereign, are tied to no religion, wife, or ſovereign. But as ſoon as they are bound by ſacramental ordinances to profeſs a certain religion; by conjugal promiſes to cleave to a certain woman; and by oaths of allegiance to ſubmit to a certain ſovereign; they are highly guilty, if they break through their engagements without a *capital* reaſon. I ſay *without a* CAPITAL *reaſon,* becauſe, as God allows divorce in caſe of *undeniable* adultery; ſo he permits our renouncing a church *undeniably* and *capitally* corrupt, and our withdrawing from a government *undeniably* and *capitally* tyrannical. I lay a peculiar emphaſis upon the words *undeniably* and *capitally,* to make room for the ſcriptural doctrine which

which you advance p. 66, " The perfonal vices of
" our governors, and any flight error in their ad-
" miniftration, will not juftify our refifting them ;"
much lefs will an *imaginary* error, or a *groundlefs* fuf-
picion do it. And of this nature are undoubtedly
the American conceits, that reafonable, legal taxes
are not *due* by fubjects to the fupreme power which
protects them; that a direct and equal reprefentation in parliament is conftitutionally neceffary to
the lawfulnefs of a money-bill; and that the Britifh
legiflature ufes the Colonifts in a tyrannical manner,
becaufe it infifts upon fatisfaction for the depredations wantonly committed by the mobbing Bof-
tonians. From the whole, I hope, I may fafely
conclude, that the foundation of Dr. Price's peculiar patriotifm is laid in a grofs miftake;—a
miftake which confifts in confounding the lawlefs liberty of a *favage*, who lives under no fort
of government, with the lawful liberty of a *fubject*, who is protected by a civil government; and
that *government*, inftead of being the *creature of
the people*, or the *refult* of a convention between
them and their rulers, is the *creature of God*, and
[when confidered in the theory] is the *caufe*, and
NOT the *refult*, of fuch a convention as the Doctor
fpeaks of.

    Page 69, You continue to quote him thus. " It
is a doctrine, which avowedly fubverts civil liberty." No: it is a doctrine, which avowedly fecures
a due fubmiffion to the governors that guard our
civil liberty.—" It reprefents mankind as a body
" of vaffals, formed to defcend like cattle from
" one fet of owners to another, who have an *ab-
" folute* dominion over them. It is a wonder, that
" thofe who view their fpecies in a light fo humi-
" liating, fhould ever be able to think of them-
" felves without regret and fhame." This argument
appears to me illogical and invidious. (1) *Illogical:*
Logick forbids us to alter the terms of a propofition.
This Dr. Price does when he fubftitutes the word
" ABSO-

" ABSOLUTE *dominion*," for REASONABLE *dominion*, which our doctrine requires. I am so far from asserting that human sovereigns have an " ABSOLUTE *dominion*" over their subjects, that I steadily oppose the pretended orthodoxy of the men, who ascribe *such* a dominion to God. I need not inform either you Sir, or Dr. Price, that there are divines in England, who teach, that God's *dominion* over his unborn creatures is so ABSOLUTE, that he not only can, but does ABSOLUTELY reprobate some of them, and appoint them to unavoidable and eternal ruin, before they hang yet at their mother's breast; nor need I remind you, that, in opposition to these men, I assert that God's sovereignty, far from being THUS *absolute*, is always circumscribed by his goodness, wisdom, and justice.—(2) The Doctor's argument is, I fear, *invidious*. What would he think of my candor, if, treading in his steps, I reflected on the subordination of wives to their husbands, soldiers to their generals, flocks to their pastors, servants to their masters, and creatures to their Creator in the same manner, in which he reflects on the subordination of subjects to their sovereigns? I shall apply his argument only to the case of married women, thus: ' The doctrine of the reasonable do-
' minion, which all husbands have over their wives, *represents womankind as a body of vassals*. And those who marry two or three husbands one after another, are *formed to descend like cattle from one owner to another, who has an* ABSOLUTE *dominion over them. It is a wonder that those, who view their* sex *in a light so humiliating, should ever be able to think of themselves without regret and shame.*'—For my part, far from being brought over to American patriotism by this logic, I think *it is a wonder*, that reasonable and good men *should ever be able to think without regret and shame*, upon the public encomiums and rewards, with which they have crowned such illogical and dangerous arguments.

The

The reſt of your quotation from Dr. Price is an
inſinuation, that arts and ſciences flouriſh no more
in a country, where the people ſubmit to a monarch who will be obeyed, whether high republicans will ſubmit or not. The whole of his argument is ſummed up in theſe concluding lines:
" With what luſtre do the ancient free ſtates of
" Greece ſhine in the annals of the world? How
" different is that country now, under the Great
" Turk? The difference between a country in-
" habited *by men*, and *by brutes*, is not greater."
—I am not for an *abſolute* monarchy. I repeat it,
the Engliſh conſtitution, which places the legiſlative power in a king, a body of patrician ſenators,
and an houſe of plebeian lawgivers, appears to me
the moſt perfect upon earth; becauſe it collects in
one political focus all the advantages of the French
monarchy, the Venetian ariſtocracy, and the new
American democracy. Neverthelefs, as a lover of
truth and matter of fact, I ſhall venture to pro-
poſe ſome queries relative to Dr. Price's inſinuation. What people are more ſelf-governed, or
more *free from ſupreme authority*, than the Hotten-
tots; and what people come nearer than they, to
the wildneſs and ſtupidity of brutes?—Were not
the Lacedemonians, with all the ado they made
about liberty, ſurpriſingly regardleſs of arts and
ſciences? Did not learning ſo flouriſh in Egypt
and Babylon, under abſolute princes, that the
Greeks formerly went there for improvement, as
we now do to our renowned univerſities?—When
did arts and ſciences flouriſh more in Judea, than
in Solomon's reign; and who ever was a more abſolute monarch?—When did they reach a higher
perfection in Rome, than under the reign of Auguſtus? And yet Auguſtus was a deſpot.—What
king ever ruled the French with an higher hand
than Lewis XIV? And was it not under his reign,
that the French literature ſhone in her meridian
glory?—When did Ruſſia emerge out of a ſea of
barbarity and rude ignorance? Was it not when
				Peter

Peter the Great, her defpotic emperor, lent her
his powerful hand? And do not at this day arts
and fciences continue to make rapid progrefs there,
under the patronage of the prefent defpotic em-
prefs?—What people are under a more abfolute government, than the Pruffians? And in what part
of Germany do the *Belles Lettres* flourifh more than
in Pruffia? If Dr. Price does thefe hints juftice,
he will own, that an high monarchical government
is at leaft as favourable to the improvement of arts
and fciences, as an high republican adminiftration.
But, I repeat it, the middle, conftitutional way is
preferable to both thofe extremes.

Page 73, You favour me with another quotation from Dr. Price. The doctrine of it centers in
the laft paragraph, which runs this. " *All dele-*
" *gated power muft be fubordinate and limited.*"
Granted. All governing power is delegated from
the King of Kings, and therefore it is fubordinate
to him, and is limited by the bounds which he
has fixed, that is, by reafon, fcripture, and the
apparent good of the people. The Doctor goes on :
" If Omnipotence can, with any fenfe, be afcrib-
" ed to a legiflature, it muft be lodged where All
" legislative power originates; that is,
" in the people."

This is a groundlefs fuppofition, which the
Doctor and you take for granted ;—a mifchievous
fuppofition, which is directly contrary to Scripture
and Reafon. And firft to Scripture. *Put them in
mind,* fays the Apoftle, to be subject *to princi-
palities and powers, to obey magiftrates.* And why
Chriftians are to be thus fubject, he informs us
where he fays, that *The powers that are, are ordained*
of God, not of the people ; and that *they who refift,
refift the ordinance of GOD,* and not of the people.
A people, who have no governors, may indeed
chufe their governors, juft as a fingle woman may
chufe a hufband : but the authority of the governors once chofen depends upon the people no more,
than the authority of a hufband depends upon his

. D   wife,

.wife, though she chose him preferably to all other men;—no more than the legislative authority of our plebeian lawgivers depends upon the freeholders or burgesses, who elected them preferably to other gentlemen.

This will probably offend our republican levellers, who fancy they are all born legislators, and can confer the power of legislation on the members of the house of commons, just as the king can confer the honour of knighthood upon a gentleman. But I must speak the truth, and do my subject justice, whoever is displeased at me for it. And I am ready to defend the following proposition against all our levellers and mistaken patriots. The people, that is, the governed, can no more create governing or legislative power, and bestow it upon the members of parliament whom they chuse, than the aldermen, who have the right of chusing a mayor, can create a mayoralty;—no more than the women, who have the right of chusing an husband, can create masculine supremacy;—no more than the servants, who have chosen a master, can create masterly power; or the soldiers, who chuse to list under this or that captain, rather than another, can create the military authority to which they submit.

You possibly reply, What, is not Edmund Burke, Esq; *my* representative? Did not I chuse him to represent *me* in parliament? Did not I invest him with *my* legislating power? And do not I, in his person, share in the government of Great Britain? Indeed you do not, Sir, any more than I partake of the royal dignity in the person of the king. Permit me to hand you out of your imaginary paradise of legislation, by the following important distinction. Every member of the house of commons has two characters. The first is that of representative of the commons of all the British empire in general, and of a certain borough or shire in particular. The second and nobler character of a member of parliament is, that of representative of God himself.

According

According to the former character, he is an agent
of the people: but with refpect to the latter, he is,
in his degree, the fubftitute of God. According
to the former capacity, he fpreads before the legiflature the wants or wifhes of the people in general,
and of his borough or fhire in particular: and according to the latter capacity he, in his degree,
makes laws, if the majority of the legiflating body
concurs with him.

Should you fay, that this is a political refinement,
which originates from my fancy, I reply, that it is a
folid diftinction which has its fource in the very nature of things: and I prove it by a parallel cafe,
which will ftrike you fo much the more as it is probably your own. The majority of a certain congregation of proteftants in Briftol, expreffed a defire to
have you for their paftor, and upon this title you
were ordained. But does it follow, that your authority to preach the gofpel afcends from your flock to
you? If your congregation infifted upon your
*preaching to them fmooth things, and prophefying de-
ceits,* becaufe they chofe you to be their minifter,
would you directly convince them of their folly, by
a diftinction fimilar to mine? Would you not fay,
Gentlemen, though I am your minifter, and though
I was ordained in confequence of your fuffrages,
yet now I am ordained, I have an authority which
you never gave nor can give. I am the minifter
of God, as well as your paftor. My commiffion to
preach the gofpel I have received from Chrift, and
NOT from you; and by order of that commiffion,
whether you will hear, or whether you will forbear,
I muft preach to you fevere as well as foothing
truths.—Apply this, Sir, to our political queftion,
and you will fee, that the members of parliament,
in their capacity of legiflators, are no more author-
ifed by the people to make laws, and bound to vote
according to the directions of their conftituents;
than you and I receive authority from our flocks
to preach the gofpel, and are bound, in the delivery
of our meffage to the people, to confult their vario is

humours; becaufe legiflators derive their authority from God, juft as gofpel minifters do their commiffion from Christ. Were this obfervation properly attended to, our lawgivers would ftudy chriftian politics with affiduity, that they might fully underftand the will of God, the fupreme lawgiver, whom they reprefent, and to whom they fhall one day give a ftrict account for the precious talent of legiflation, with which they are entrufted : and Dr. Price would no longer poifon the minds of thoufands, with the antichriftian doctrine, that every man is, or ought to be, his own legiflator, and that legiflative power afcends from the people, and governing power from the governed.

(2) As this notion is contrary to fcripture, fo is it to *reafon*. For reafon dictates, that if governing power came from the people, the people might, whenever they pleafe, chufe to difobey their governors, and would have a *right* to do fo. A parallel cafe will make you fenfible of the truth of this affertion. Supreme, legiflative authority belongs to *me* within the narrow compafs of my family, as you fuppofe that it belongs to *the people* throughout the wide extent of the British dominions. I may, if I pleafe, delegate to my fervant the right of making houfehold-regulations. And if I had delegated my right, and in confequence of this delegation my fervant commanded me to breakfaft at eight o'clock, is it not evident, that, if I pleafed, I might inftantly refume my delegated power, and fay, You are only my reprefentative ; my authority exceeds yours ; I infift upon breakfafting an hour later. Leaving the application of my fimile to your good fenfe, I conclude, that, whenever you and Dr. Price teach, that the power of the governors originates from, or is delegated by, the governed, you fap the foundation of all government, and indirectly bring in the lawlefs democracy, which a facred hiftorian defcribes where he fays, *In thofe days there was no king in Ifrael: Every man did that which was right in his own eyes.*

But

But the Doctor adds, " *For* THEIR [the people's] " *fakes government was inftituted; and their's is the* " *only real Omnipotence !*" And what if it is, does this prove that governing power is delegated by the governed? Would not the meaneft corporation in the kingdom difhonour itfelf, if it complimented me for faying, Military *government is inftituted for the fake* of foldiers, and *theirs is the only real omnipotence* of the army : Therefore the power of the general and other officers is delegated by, and originates from *the foldiers*. Equally conclufive, O ye American patriots, is your grand argument concerning the origin of power !

Page 76, Introducing the Doctor for the laft time, you fay, ' To prove the right Great Britain has to ' tax America, it is very common to plead, We ' are the PARENT STATE. - Hear Dr. Price upon ' this fubject.'—" Thefe are the magic words, " which have fafcinated and mifled us.—The Eng- " lifh came from *Germany*. Does that give the *Ger-* " *man* ftates a right to tax us ?" To this triumphant queftion I anfwer, No : becaufe the *Germans* do not protect us : But if the *German* Diet had, to this day, kept up fleets to guard our coafts, and an army to fight our battles : and if we had always called the Emperor of Germany *our fovereign*, had received his lieutenants as *our governors*, and admitted his coin as *our lawful* money, I would think it a great piece of difloyalty and injuftice, to refufe him a reafonable tribute. For protection, and reafonable taxes, are equivalent to each other, as the cuftomer's money is equivalent to the tradef-man's goods. Nor is it lefs unreafonable in the Colonifts, who have got their immenfe wealth under the protective wings of Great Britain, to refufe Great Britain the return of reafonable taxes, now they are able to pay them ; than it would be in you to receive the goods of a mercer, and to refufe making him a proper acknowledgment by paying

the reafonable bill he fends you, when he thinks
you can difcharge it without diftreffing yourfelf.
And as it would be a fhameful excufe in a gentleman, to fay to his tradefmen, who kindly delayed
fending in their bills till he had received his rents,
Why did you not fend me your bills before? So it
is an unjuft excufe in the Colonifts to fay to the
protective power, Why did you not pafs bills of
internal taxation before the ftamp-act? For a juft
right, founded on the eternal nature and fitnefs of
things, can never be loft, tho' it fhould never be
exercifed. If you pay your fervant wages for fifty
years, without ever commanding him to go on one
fingle errand, and at laft order him to do fomething which he is able to do; he cannot plead pre-
fcription with any decency. He would betray an
ingratitude equal to his infolence if he faid, Sir,
you never commanded me to go on your errands
before, and therefore you have loft your claim to
my obedience. Had fuch a fervant a grain of mo-
defty and duty, he would argue in a manner diame-
trically oppofite: he would fay, I am doubly bound
to go on all your errands to the utmoft of my power.
Your not calling upon me to exert my ftrength for
you before, lays me under a double obligation to do
it now with chearfulnefs.

This brings to my mind another curious argument
of Dr. Price. "Had the colonies [fays he] been
"communities of *foreigners*, over whom we wanted
"to acquire dominion, &c. they [fome Englifhmen]
"are ready to admit that their refiftance would have
"been juft. In my opinion, this is the fame with
"faying, that the Colonies ought to be *worfe off*
"than the reft of mankind, becaufe they are our
"*Brethren*." To fhew the inconclufivenefs of this
argument, I need only bring it to open light thus:
You have more right to command your own children
and fervants, than to command ftrangers: And therefore your own children and fervants are *worfe off* than
ftrangers: Or thus: The Britifh legiflature has more
right to tax Britifh fubjects than the fubjects of *France*
and Spain: And therefore Britifh fubjects are
worfe

worfe off than Frenchmen and Spaniards. — The
fubjects of France and Spain would juftly rife againft
Britifh taxation, and therefore the fubjects of Great-
Britain may alfo juftly rife againft it.—Or thus:
Englifhmen have more authority over their wives,
than over the wives of the Turks; therefoie Englifh
women *are worfe off than the reft of womankind,* yea
than the wives of the Turks, *becaufe they are* our
wives? I am grieved to fee a doctor in divinity
proftitute by fuch arguments, chriftianity, morality,
and logic to the infatuation of a reftlefs, levelling
patriotifm.

The preceding argument of Dr. Price is introduced by the levelling propofition which follows.

"Unlefs different parts of the fame community
"are united by an equal representation, all
fuch authority" [*that is all the authority exercifed by one part of the community over the other*] "is inconfiftent with the principles of civil liberty,"—*and*
"cannot be diftinguifhed from the fervitude " of
one" *part* " to another." If this doctrine is true,
are not the Lord Mayor, the aldermen, and the freemen of the city of London, chargeable with tyranny;
as well as the king, the parliament, and the electors
of Great-Britain? Is not Middlefex filled with flaves,
as well as America? And may I not addrefs the London patriots thus? Gentlemen, If Dr. Price's levelling doctrine is *falfe,* why do you honour and reward
him for propagating it? And if it is *true,* why do you
not follow it? Why do you not begin to level authority in your own jurifdiction, as you want the
king and parliament to do in theirs? In a word,
why do you not *unite the different parts of* your com-
munity, by an equal representation? Your
community is made up of two forts of men: Freemen, and men who have not the freedom of your
city. Thefe, who make by far the greater part of
your community, have no fhare in the government
of it. By keeping the right of legiflating for the city
in your own hands, you exclude them from an e-
qual representation; and according to the admired principles of your champion, your *authority*

cannot be diftinguifbed from the fervitude of one part of the city *to the other,*—from the fervitude of the non-free-men to yourfelves ; and therefore you yourfelves are as much involved in the guilt of enflaving your fellow-creatures, as your fcheme fuppofes the king and parliament to be. Let your principles of civil liberty take place at home : Level authority in the *city*; or for decency's fake, never more reflect upon our legiflators, becaufe they do not level it in the *empire.*

Dr. Price prefents us with another bold plea for levelling patriotifm ; and it is fo much the more curious, as it is a perfect jeft upon the freedom of the city of London, with which the patriots have prefented him, This plea runs thus : " We [non-" voters] fubmit to a parliament that does not " reprefent us, and therefore they [the Colo-" nifts] ought. How ftrange an argument is this? " It is faying we want liberty, and therefore " they ought to want it. Suppofe it true, that " they are indeed contending for a better conftitu-" tion of government, and more liberty than we en-" joy : Ought this to make us angry?—Is it gene-" rous, becaufe we are in a fink, to endeavour to " draw them into it ? Ought we not rather to wifh " earneftly that there may be at leaft ONE FREE " COUNTRY left upon earth, to which we may fly " when venality, luxury, and vice, have completed " the ruin of liberty here?"—I own to you, Sir, that if I were the author of Dr. Price's *Obferva-tions,* and the patriots of London rewarded me for my book, by giving me the freedom of their city, I I would reject that honour with deteftation, and fay : Gentlemen, what do you mean by prefent-ing me with the *freedom* of your city? Is not your intended favour a glaring proof that you en-flaved me before, as you do all my fellow-citi-zens who are not freemen ? Will you make me a partaker of your fin ? Will you bribe me into

tyranny.

tyranny by a gold box? Far from accepting a place in your partial legiflature, I will excite my enflaved fellow-citizens to rife againft you. I will *contend for a better conftitution of* city-*government, and more liberty than we enjoy:* Ought *this to make you angry? Is it generous, becaufe* the non-freemen *are in a fink, to endeavour to* keep *them in it? Ought you not rather to wifh earneftly, that there may at leaft be* ONE FREE City *left in* Great-Britain, *to which we may fly, when venality, luxury, and vice have compleated the ruin of liberty* in the kingdom? Till Dr. Price acts in this manner, and the city-patriots recant their encomiums of his book, or abolifh the diftinction between *free-men* and *non-freemen* in their community; they muft give the unprejudiced world leave to confider them as inconfiftent men, who fay and do not;—as partial men, who lay upon other communities heavy burdens, which they will not fuffer their own community to touch;—and as reftlefs, imperious fubjects, who infift upon our legiflators levelling authority in America, when they themfelves will not level it in England; no not in the city of London, where American patriotifm has fet up its ftandard. But I return to taxes.

You will perhaps object, that, If the Coloniffs once owed taxes to the Britifh legiflature for protection, yet they owe them now no more; becaufe all ties and natural contracts are now broken; the mother-country having turned her protection into acts of open hoftility: I reply, that Great Britain chaftifes the Colonies for their difobedience, with the reluctance of a fond parent, who, when fhe corrects an undutiful child, is ready to take his part againft a murderer. Were it not for the terror of our fleets, fome greedy European powers would perhaps at this very time fall upon the Colonies, and endeavour to annex them to their dominions.—Again: If your fervant or your fon had abufed you, and you gave him correction to bring him to a fenfe of his duty; would he not

add

red folly to wickedness if he faid: Sir, my obligation to obey you ceafes: For inftead of ufing me
as a mafter, or a father, you prepare to correct me ;
nay, you ftrike me! Every relation therefore, is
now at an end between us. You have cut the laft
knot which tied me to you, and I will now fight
you as an open enemy.—This immoral excufe
brings to my remembrance the obftinacy of fome in-
corrigible men, whom David defcribes thus : *The
wrath of God came upon them* fo their difobedience,
and flew the fatteft of them. For all this they finned
ftill—Yea, *they finned yet more againft him,*—their divine fovereign. But I hope better things of our pious American brethren. Notwithftanding the un-
wearied endeavours of fome patriots, to confirm
them in their unnatural refiftance, they will, I truft,
fubmit to God and the king.

Page 76, you continue to quote the Doctor thus:
" Children having no property, and being incapa-
" ble of guarding themfelves, the author of na-
" ture has committed the care of them to their
" parents, and fubjected them to their abfolute au-
" thority. But there is a period when, having
" acquired property, and a capacity of judging for
" themfelves, they become independent agents ;
" and when, for this reafon, the authority of their
" parent ceafes, and becomes nothing, but the
" refpect and influence due to benefactors." This
argument is as illogical as it is ingenious. The
flaw of it confifts in confounding the double relation which the Colonifts fuftain, namely that of
fons, and that of *fubjects* of Great Britain : Granting therefore, to Dr. Price, that according to the
law of nature, there is a time when *children* become independent by acquiring property and wifdom ; yet this is not the cafe with refpect to subr-
jects ; but whatever be their wealth and age, and
whatever capacity they have of judging for themfelves, they continue to be *dependent* agents ; being
ftill bound to obey, in all *reafonable* things, the
legiflative power under which providence has placed
                                                  them.

them. The plaufible argument of your fecond, when touched with the finger of found logick, fhrinks therefore into a fophifm as glaring as that which follows: When the Prince of Wales fhall be of age, he fhall be *independent* on his *father*, and therefore he fhall alfo be *independent* on the *king.* He fhall have the liberty of taking a ride whether *his father* confent or not, and therefore he fhall alfo have the liberty of commanding the fleet and the army whether *his king* confent or not. If you would be frighted at my wickednefs, were I to ftir up the prince to rebellion by fuch fophiftry; why do you recommend as "excellent," a pamphlet which fupports the American revolt by fo weak an argument.

You continue to quote the Doctor. "Suppofing, "therefore, that the order of nature in eftablifh-"ing the relation between parents and children, "ought to have been the rule of our conduct to "the Colonies, we *fhould have been gradually* re-"laxing our authority as they grew up." Another great miftake this, of which you will be fenfible if you apply the Doctor's fimile to the cafe in hand, thus: If the fovereign ought to confider the Colonifts as the children of Great Britain, and to treat them in a parental manner; *as they grew up* in power he *fhould have been gradually* leffening their burdens. But is not the inference big with abfurdity? Becaufe parents lay no burden upon a fucking child, does it follow they are to lay gradu-ally lefs and lefs upon him *as he grows up?* Does not every unprejudiced perfon fee that, if a parent want his children's affiftance, he may increafe, and has a right, as they grow up, gradually to increafe, the little burdens which he wants them to carry; and that nothing would be more abfurd than " *gra-* " *dually to relax his authority*" in this refpect, when their increafing ftrength begins to render that *au-thority* valuable? But fuppofing *parents* ought to require lefs and lefs of their *children* as they grow up, does it follow that SOVEREIGNS ought to do fo

too with refpeçt to their subjects? Is there a
legiflature in all the univerfe, fo far funk in ftupi-
dity as to fay to their fubjeéts, You have paid taxes to the fovereign for above a thoufand years, you
are now grown up into an ancient kingdom; the
American patriots have infinuated, that as our
fubjeéts are our children, we *fhould gradually relax
our authority* of taxing them *as they grow up*, and
therefore we enaét that you fhall pay but one half
of our taxes for fifty years, and in a hundred years
you fhall pay nothing, for the government will be
old enough to fupport itfelf without any taxes at
all : So fhall we fhew the world, that we are grey-
headed lawgivers, that you " are no children,"
and that our once childifh conftitution is grown
to manly wifdom and ftrength. Such are the rea-
fonings of Dr. Price's " moft excellent pamphlet !"
Can feathers be lighter than thefe arguments with
which the American patriots hope to batter down
Britifh patriotifm ! Feathers however may do mifchief, when they are clofely compaéted in a ftrong
paper-vehicle; when they are rendered ponderous
by the weight of a gold box, and when bufy prejudice hurls them through town and country with in-
credible ardor.

This part of the American controverfy is fo important, that I beg leave to throw light upon it by
an appofite illuftration. I live in a parifh, where
the wealth of feveral men confifts in the number
and ftrength of their children. A poor collier has,
it may be, five or fix fons. He works night and
day to maintain them, in hopes that they will one
day help to maintain him, and borrows money to
build an houfe; flattering himfelf that by the affiftance of his children, as they grow up, he fhall foon
difcharge the debt. When they are eight years of
age, they get him a groat a day; at fourteen, a fhilling; and at nineteen, eighteen-pence; fo that the
poor man has a fair profpeét of being foon, as he
fays, " on a level with the world." But alas! his
hope proves abortive : A bufy body, an envious
neighbour

neighbour, or fome defigning perfon, poifons the minds of his dutiful children with the politicks of Dr. Price, and fays, Your father does not ufe you well. He is a tyrant. The ftronger you grow, the more burdens he lays upon you; whereas he fhould lay lefs and lefs. You " are no children :" You can maintain yourfelves, and fpend your own money. If I were in your place, this very day I would leave the old man, and fet up for myfelf.—Too many of thefe deluded youths have I feen, firft, ufing their parent ill through fuch mifchievous infinuations ; and then turning their backs upon him, to go and fquander in riot and bloody fports, the money which they fhould have applied to the difcharge of the family-debt, which was contracted to build the houfe, where they have lived rent-free all their life.

If I blame this conduct in my young, undutiful parifhioners, can I approve of it in my American fellow-fubjects, who defpife a legiflative power poffeffed of *royal*, as well as *parental* authority ? Is it right in them to turn their backs upon their mother-country, when fhe groans under the weight of a debt, which has been in part contracted for their fake ? And can we wonder enough at the conduct of Dr. Price, who tells us of " the ruin " with which the national debt threatens us ;—a " debt much heavier than that which fifty years " ago, the wifeft men thought would neceffarily " fink us ;" an immenfe debt, which we have no fair profpect of difcharging but by the prudent management of growing taxes, and by the loyal filial and brotherly affiftance, which we have a right to expect from the Colonies; can we, I fay, wonder enough at the ftrange conduct of Dr. Price, who while he tries to frighten us with the awful afpect of this national debt, fays all he can to render us odious and contemptible to the Colonies, by whofe friendly and proportionable help we are in hopes of difcharging it ?

This

This conduct of Dr. Price is so much the more surprising, as he intimates in his conclusion, that " The debt of England, &c. might be acknow- " ledged the debt of every individual part of the " whole empire, Asia, as well as *America* includ- " ed." For my part, supposing *subjects* had a right to retire from their *sovereigns*, as grown up children have to leave their parents ; I do not see how the Colonies could in conscience desire to set up for themselves, and form a separate empire, before they have helped their mother-country to extricate herself out of the difficulty of her national debt : nor can I conceive how the sovereign could justly permit them to commence independent; be- cause the strength and wealth of *all* the British empire are the double *security* on which thousands of people have placed either the whole or a part of their fortune in the stocks ; and it would be wronging the public to let so considerable a part of that *security*, as America, be lost.

However [says Dr. Price, who is always unhap- pily ingenious in finding fault with the sovereign's conduct] " Had we nourished and favoured Ame- " rica, with a view to commerce, instead of con- " sidering it as a country to be governed, &c. a " growing surplus in the revenue might have been " gained, which, invariably applied to the gradual " discharge of the national debt, would have de- " livered us from the ruin with which it threatens " us."—" This trade" [with the Colonies] " was " not only an *increasing trade*; but it was a trade " *in which we had no rivals*; a trade *certain*, *con-* " *stant*, and *uninterrupted*."

But why was this trade " *an increasing trade*, *in* *which we had no rivals?*" Was it not because the Colonists were so taken up with clearing ground, planting, and building, that they had no time to apply themselves to the culture of less necessary arts? But now that their houses are built, their fields in proper order, and their numbers multi- plying fast, they must either idly look one at an- other

other, or erect manufactures, and provide themselves
with an hundred articles, with which they have
hitherto been supplied from England. So shall they
themselves, naturally become our " rivals" in manufactures: and the moment this is the case, our
trade with them will naturally *decreasc*, and Dr.
Price's scheme for discharging the national debt will
prove an idle speculation, unless we should act so
tyrannical a part as to put a total stop to industry
among them. Hence appears the propriety and necessity of *internal* taxes, in order to obtain from them
a revenue, which may be at once rational, scriptural
constitutional and *sure.*

Again : Why has our trade with the Colonies
been hitherto " *a trade certain, constant, and un-*
" *interrupted ?*" Was it not because Great Britain
by maintaining her *supremacy* over the Colonies,
could confine their trade, and make it flow in
British channels? If she gives up her *supremacy,*
will she be able to oblige the Colonies to trade with
her, more than with France, Holland, or Spain? Is
it not evident, that in the same year in which she
loses her *supremacy,* not only her American dominions and taxes, but likewise her American ports and
trade will be lost for ever, unless the Colonists can
get more by us than by other nations? I should wonder, that so obvious a thought escaped so penetrating
a genius as Dr. Price; if I did not know, that the
peculiar patriotism, which I oppose, is so intent upon looking for defects in the constitution, and for
blemishes in our governors, that it frequently over-
looks the most glaring truths.

Return we now to your quotation, and let us see
if the conclusion is preferable to the beginning:
Dr. Price goes on. " But, like *mad* parents, we
" have done the contrary ; and at the very time
" when our authority should have been most re-
" laxed, we have carried it to the greatest extent,
" and exercised it with the greatest rigor. *No*
" *wonder then,* that they [the Colonies] have
" turned upon us ; and obliged us to remember,
                                        " that

" that they are not children." Bring the Doctor's meaning to open light : unfold his argument, and you will find the following propositions, which may be confidered as the political creed of Dr. Price and the American patriots. (1) Parents who do not relax their authority of laying fome eafy burdens upon their children, as their children grow more able to bear fuch burdens, are " mad parents."—(2) Our political parents, that is, our legiflators, who have not relaxed their authority of laying fome eafy taxes upon their American children, as thefe children grew more able to pay fuch taxes, are " *mad*" legiflators.—(3) When children grow up, and have got ftrength enough to bear a little burden for their heavy-laden parents ; and when fuch parents defire their children to give them fome filial affiftance, it is *no wonder* that grown up children *turn upon* their parents, and *oblige* them " *to remember that they are not children.*"—(4) The Colonies have now got ftrength enough to eafe Great Britain by bearing fome fmall proportion of the taxes with which fhe is loaded :: and therefore it is *no wonder that they turn,* fword in hand, *upon* their mother country, and *oblige her to remember that they are not children.* Such is the manner in which a doctor in divinity enforces the fifth commandment !

If this doctrine fhocks you, Sir, what would you think of it, were I to apply it to the character of subjects of Great Britain ;—a character this, which the Colonifts bear, as well as that of *Sons of Britons?* In this view of things, the Doctor's patriotic creed naturally fwells with the following articles. (1) A fovereign who does not relax his authority of laying reafonable taxes upon his *fubjects,* as they grow more able to pay fuch taxes, acts like a " *mad*" fovereign. (2) When fubjects have got ftrength and wealth enough to pay fuch taxes, they may " *turn upon* " their Sovereign, and *oblige him to remember, that they are no impotent fubjects.* And laftly, to make an application of

the

the whole, the king and parliament have acted like *mad* lawgivers, by laying a reasonable tax upon their American subjects; and the Colonists only oppose *madness*, when they rise up in arms against their sovereign, rather than pay the reasonable tax laid upon them. If there is a grain of piety, morality, or good sense in one article of this patriotic creed, I consent to forfeit my claim to a grain of common sense.

Dr. Price may possibly attempt to prove, that the last articles of this creed do not belong to his doctrine: For he insinuates, that the Colonists are not the subjects of Great Britain. Take his own words : " The people of America are no more the " subjects of the people of Great Britain, than the " people of Yorkshire are the subjects of the peo- " ple of Middlesex." This proposition is true, if the Doctor by *the people of Great Britain* means *you, me*, and our *British fellow-subjects*. But who ever pretended that the Colonists are the subjects of Yorkshiremen or Cornishmen ? No Briton but the king can say to a Colonist, You are *my* subject. And if *George* the Third has a right to say it, to every Colonist, it is only as he is the head and representative of the whole legislative power, and can say it to every Englishman. When we assert, that the Colonists are *the subjects of Great Britain*, we do not set ourselves above them : We only mean that they are under the legislative power of Great Britain, as well as we. And Dr. Price inad- vertently grants it, when he adds, " They are our " *fellow subjects:*" For if they are our *fellow- subjects*, they are bound to obey the British legis- lature as much as we are; as much at least as the body of the non-voters in England; a countless body this, which far exceeds the number of all the American Colonists, as appears from the ac- count which Dr. Price himself gives us of the inequality of our representation, and the prodigi- ous difference which the constitution makes. be- tween Briton and Briton, with regard to the pri- vilege

vilege of voting at elections. "In Great Britain,"
[fays he] " confifting of near fix millions of in-
" habitants, 5723 perfons, moft of them the low-
" eft of the people, elect one half of the houfe
" of commons; 364 votes chufe the ninth part."
According to this account, and that which in another place he gives us of the Colonies, which,
he fays, confift of " near three millions of people,"
it follows that when the parliament taxes the
non-voters in England, it taxes at leaft two millions
of perfons more than when it taxes all Britifh
America.

With refpect to the prerogative which Britons,
as a more ancient people enjoy, when they chufe
parliament-men; it may be as reafonably and legally invefted in an elder community of fubjects, as
a family-prerogative is invefted in an elder brother. Add to this, that by paying heavier taxes,
we now make, and, I hope, fhall always equita-
bly make a compenfation to the Colonies for the
fuperior privileges annexed to our *eldership*. Nor
is it more juft in the Colonies to levy war againft
Britons on the prefent occafion, than it would be
in younger brothers to fall fword in hand upon their
elder brother, becaufe cuftom and law allow him peculiar rights neceffary to fupport the dignity of their
family, which, as the firft-born fon, he *peculiarly*
reprefents.

Should you fay, that, according to this doctrine,
the Colonifts lofe the birth-right tranfmitted to
them, as fons of free-born Englifhmen, namely,
the right of being *their own legiflators* : A facred
right this, " without which government is a
curfe;" and fubjection, " abject flavery".—I reply, that what the people of England never had,
cannot be loft by the people of England, much
lefs by the people of America.—" What! [fays
your fcheme] have not the voters in England the
right of making their own laws?" No, Sir, no
more than Angels in heaven and Frenchmen on
earth.—" What! Do we not chufe our own
repre-

reprefentatives? And are not our reprefentative*
lawgivers?" Yes, Sir, but they are not lawgivers
as they are our agents and reprefentatives ; but as
they are the agents and reprefentatives of the
Great Lawgiver, who *ordains the Powers that are.*
—" However they legiflate in confequence of our
" choice." True; but not thro' any legiflative
power communicated to them by virtue of our
choice. You rule your own wife, if you have one,
in confequence of the choice fhe made of you for
an hufband; but not by any authority fhe conveyed to you. If you have fons, and give them their
choice of half a dozen mafters; he whom they
chufe, acquires a right to command them in confequence of their choice, but not thro' any authority conveyed to him by virtue of that choice.
The authority of commanding your fons muft
come from an higher fource than their election.
If they could beftow magifterial authority, they
could refume it as often as they are inclined to play
the truant.—" What! according to the Britifh
conftitution, is it not the prerogative of certain
men, whom we call *freeholders* and *burgeffes*, to give
their vote to certain gentlemen, who, in confequence of thofe votes, are admitted as members of
the houfe of commons, in which a large fhare of the
legiflative power is lodged?" True: This is a
peculiarity of the Britifh government, juft as it is
a peculiarity of the church of England, that fome
men called *rectors, vicars,* and *patrons,* can give a
ftudent in divinity a title, in confequence of which
he is invefted with authority to be an embaffador
of Chrift, and to preach the gofpel. But obferve!
this authority comes not from his *rector, vicar,* or
patron: It defcends from CHRIST himfelf. If I
fancied, that authority to preach the gofpel originates from *me,* becaufe I can give a candidate for
orders a title, in confequence of which he may be
admitted into holy orders, and preach *for* me, and
to me; I fhould betray my fpiritual vanity in the
church, as much as thofe men betray their political

cal pride in the ſtate, who fancy that they are born
legiſlators, and that they can convey the power of
making laws to the gentlemen for whom they vote
at an election, juſt as you can convey the authority of dreſſing your horſe, to the man whom you
chuſe for your groom.   I have dwelt the more upon this part of our controverſy, becauſe the notion
that *ſelf-government* and *ſelf-legiſlation* naturally belong to all men in general, and to the people and
Colonies of Great Britain in particular, is the πρωτον
ψευδος, the capital error, from which flows your
American patriotiſm. The moment that error is diſ-
covered, this boaſted virtue viſibly degenerates into
a vice compounded of one or more of the following
ingredients, inattention, prejudice, ignorance, conceit, pride, ambition, envy, refractorineſs, and civil antinomianiſm.

We have ſeen in the preceding letter, how
greatly you have wronged the ſovereign in pointing
out the cauſe of the war with America ; let us ſee
if Dr. Price does the king and parliament more
juſtice than you do. " The preſent conteſt [ſays
" his pamphlet] is for dominion on the ſide of
" the Colonies, as well as on ours :—But with this
" difference. WE are ſtruggling for dominion
" over OTHERS ; THEY for SELF-dominion; the
" nobleſt of all bleſſings.—I am perſuaded, that
" were pride, and the luſt of dominion, extermi-
" nated from every heart among us, &c. this
" quarrel would ſoon be ended—To ſheath our
" ſwords in the bowels of our brethren—for no
" other end than to oblige them to acknowledge
" our ſupremacy : how horrid!—This is the cur-
" ſed ambition that led a Cæſar, and an Alexan-
" der, and many other mad conquerors, to attack
" peaceful communities, and to lay waſte the
" earth.—This war can have no other object than
" the extenſion of power." Theſe patriotic aſ-
ſertions appear to me big with abſurdity and
groſs injuſtice. Does Great Britain aim at an " *ex-
" tenſion of power*," when ſhe protects our injured
merchants,

merchants, her oppreſſed ſubjects? Have not all
ſovereigns the right to defend wronged innocence?
Nay, is it not their bounden duty ſo to do with
reſpect to their own ſubjects? Does our legiſlature
" extend her power," when ſhe taxes the Americans? Has not Dr. Price himſelf granted that they
were taxed in the late reign? And does not his
own conſcience declare, that protective powers
have the right of reaſonably taxing the protected;
and that this right has been enjoyed by all ſovereigns
in all ages?

Again: If the king of Great Britain is the lawful ſovereign of the Colonies,. and has as much
right to command them as command us;—if all
the men in power among them before the revolt,
took OATHS OF FIDELITY to him, as the king of
Great Britain, who is inſeparably connected with
his Britiſh parliament;—and if they have always
ſubmitted to Britiſh laws, and " *always looked to this
country as their home*"—if this is the caſe, I ſay,
can any thing be more unreaſonable and unjuſt
than to pour floods of odium upon the efforts, which
the ſovereign makes to bring back the Colonies to
their former allegiance; and to compare thoſe efforts to the *luſt of power*, which intoxicated Cæſar
and Alexander, when, without any provocation,
they attacked and conquered foreign kingdoms?
If a ſecond *Ket* aroſe in England, affected indepen-
dency, played the tyrant, drew all the country people from their work, and engaged half a dozen coun-
ties to revolt; would any man, except an American
patriot, dare to ſay, that it would be " *ſavage folly
to addreſs the throne*" for the ſuppreſſion of the
growing miſchief? Could you inſinuate with candor,
that, if the king exerted his power on ſuch an occaſion, he would act the part of a " *mad con-
queror?*" And would not your blood run cold, if
you heard a chriſtian Doctor put this wild plea in
the mouth of *Ket* and his adherents : O king, *the
ſpirit of domination*, and the *luſt of power* make thee
mad. Thou wilt *ſheath* thy *ſword in* our *bowels,*
　　　　　　　　　　　　　　　　　　　　and

and spread misery among a happy people for no other end than to oblige them to acknowledge thy supremacy. We confess that the present contest is for dominion on our side as well as on thine; but with this essential difference: Thou art struggling for dominion over OTHERS; WE *for* SELF *dominion the noblest of all blessings?*

This seditious sophism is sufficient to fill us with a just detestation of Dr. Price's politicks. But a scheme which has a direct tendency so to level authority, as to subvert all government, and abolish all subordination in the universe—such a scheme, I say, cannot be too strongly opposed: It should be totally extirpated. Archimedes said once, " Give me a point, on which I may fix my engine, and I will move the earth out of it's place: And I may say, Give me Dr. Price's political principles, and I will move all kings out of their thrones, and all subjection out of the world. To convince you of the truth of this assertion, I need only work a moment his patriotic engine in your presence.

The collector of the land tax is at the door; Fired with Dr. Price's patriotism, I run to him and say: Sir, I am a *freeman.* You shall treat me neither as a *beast,* nor as a *slave.* I never yet chose a parliament-man in all my life: Nor will I be taxed till I am directly and adequately represented in parliament. And suppose I were, I could not in conscience pay taxes to maintain a government, which enslaves millions of my free-born fellow-creatures, who are taxed without being directly or adequately represented. Besides, I pay parish rates, and the levies of my hundred; and *must I submit to be triple-taxed? Will those who send you insist upon such a supremacy over me, as will leave me nothing that I can call my own?—Would you let me alone, and suffer me to enjoy in security my property, and parish government, instead of disturbing me, I would thank and bless you.*—But if you will not, I *have a right to emancipate myself as soon as I can:* I will shew you, that I and my hundred *have the right of*
legislating

legiflating for ourfelves. This bleffing, when loft, we have always a right to refume: And I refume it now in the name of all the non-electors in the parifh and hundred, who are the majority, and who fhould be as glad as myfelf to pay taxes only when they have a mind. *Dulce pro* parochia *mori!* But fuppofe they chufe to be enflaved, I do not. Dr. Price has converted me to Patriotifm. I act according to his admired doctrine, which is fummed up in the following propofitions. " *In a free ftate* EVERY MAN *is* HIS OWN *legiflator.*"—" *To be free, is to be guided by* ONE'S OWN *will: And to be guided by the will* OF ANOTHER *is the character of* SERVITUDE."—"*As far as, in* ANY INSTANCE, *the operation of* ANY CAUSE, *comes in to reftrain the power of* SELF-GOVERNMENT," (whether it be in an individual, in a parifh, hundred, colony, province, principality, or kingdom,) " *fo far* SLAVERY *is introduced: Nor do I think that a precifer idea than this of* LIBERTY *or* SLAVERY *can be formed.* According to this doctrine, I can not only refufe paying taxes with the majority of my hundred, but alone, by virtue of my own perfonal right. For if EVERY MAN *is* HIS OWN *legiflator,* it is plain, that he can make his own laws. Now, as I am a man, I am my own legiflator; and as fuch I enact, that I ought not to pay the tax you demand of me. Should you fay, that the parliament has enacted I fhall pay it, I reply [in Mr. Evans's and Dr. Price's words] *What a man has is* ABSOLUTELY *his own: No man has a right to take it from him without his confent, expreffed by himfelf, or by his own reprefentative,* i. e. by a reprefentative of his own chufing. What authority has the parliament to cede my property? " *Such a ceffion being inconfiftent with the unalienable rights of human nature, either binds not at all; or binds only the individuals who made it,*" and the men who chofe fuch individuals for their reprefentatives. This is not all: Dr. Price afferts that " *all taxes are* FREE GIFTS." And can any thing be more abfurd than to demand a FREE GIFT, as if it were a *juft debt;*
efpecially

efpecially confidering that I never promifed fuch a
gift, no nor the majority of the parifh, the hundred,
the county, or the kingdom to which I belong; the
majority not having fent any member to parliament?
A *free* gift is to be given *freely*; and whoever will
take it from us agai nft our own will, contradicts himfelf, tries to *enflave us*, *flabs our vitals*, and *commits
robbery.* And is not fuch a *grofs abufe* of power fufficient to *roufe* me *into refiftance?* Befides, why fhould
I be fo much afraid of railing a rebellion? Does not
Dr. Price fay, " He who will examine the hiftory
" of the world will find, there has generally been
" more reafon for complaining that they have been
" too patient, than that they have been turbulent
" and rebellious?" Should you object that, upon
upon this footing, all the non-voters will foon rife
againft the voters and their reprefentatives, and that
the *unity* of the kingdom will be broken? I reply in
the Doctor's pious language, " If in order to pre-
" ferve *unity*, one half of it" [the realm] " muft be
" enflaved to the other half, let it, in the name of
" God, want unity."—" Of fuch liberty, as I have
" now defcribed, it is impoffible that there fhould be
" an excefs." And I apply to your tyrannical demand the patriotic query, which he makes with
refpect to the Sovereign's claims on the province of
Maffachufet's Bay. " Can there be any Englifhmen,
" who, were it his own cafe, would not fooner lofe
" his heart's blood, than yield to claims fo pregnant
" with evils, and deftructive to every thing, that
" can diftinguifh a *freeman* from a *flave?*

Nothing can exceed the wickednefs of this patriotic fpeech of mine about taxes, except the infolence of that which follows. I fuppofe, it was made
by Satan to the Son of God, when, according to
Milton's fancy, they encountered each other in the
heavenly plains. I meet thee in the field [fays the
fiend] to defend my freedom, and affert the liberty
of thefe heavenly legions. Before I pierce thy fide
with my fpear, let me pierce thy confcience with
my

my arguments. " *In a free flate* [much more in heaven, where liberty is perfect] *every* one *is his own legiflator. To be free, is to be guided by one's own will; and to be guided by the will of another, is the character of fervitude.*" They call thee MESSIAH THE PRINCE; but for as much as thou fayeft, *I do nothing of myfelf,* and art not afhamed to add, *Father,* NOT MY *will, but thine be done;* and to teach the mean Spirits who follow thee to pray, THY WILL *be done in heaven and on earth;* it is plain, that thou " *reftraineft the power of* SELF GOVERNMENT," and " *introduceft* SLAVERY." Thou art loft to all fenfe of heavenly patriotifm. Enflaved thyfelf, thou comeft to damp the noble flame of liberty, which glows in thefe angelical bofoms; and to make us wear the badge of the moft abject flavery as thou doft. —Thou proud and bafe tool of tyranny! —Can thy reafon blame us for our noble ftruggle, fince we are not allowed to have our natural *right of legiflating for ourfelves?* And if thofe daftardly fpirits, who compofe thy hofts, fay, " *Neither have moft of us;*" I reply, " *Then you fo far want liberty, and your language is, we are not free, why will they be free?*" —" *I have no other notion of flavery, but being bound by a law, to which I do not confent.*" Now I do not confent to the law which fays, Thou fhalt obey thy divine fovereign, and honour thy heavenly father: I never made *that* law. And fuppofe I and my legions had made it, we have a right to repeal it. For "*Government is an inftitution for the benefit of the* " *people governed, which they have power to model as* " *they pleafe.*"—" *Liberty may be enjoyed in every poffible degree.*"—" *Liberty is moft compleat and per-* " *fect, when the people have moft of a fhare in go-* " *vernment, and of a controling power over the per-* " *fons, by whom it is adminiftered.*" Now thou, and thy father, are the perfons, by whom heavenly government is adminiftered. *A fpirit of domination,* and *luft of power kindle thee into rage. The only ob-ject of the war* thou wageft againft us, *is the exten-fion of dominion.* Thou wilt *maintain* thy ufurped

E   *fupremacy*

fupremacy over us : and we will maintain our native or acquired fupremacy over ourfelves. *The prefent contefl is for dominion on* thy *fide, as well as ours :* but [like a tyran'] thou art ftruggling *for dominion over* OTHERS : *and* we [like free fpirits] are ftruggling *for* SELF-*dominion, the noblefl of all bleffings.*— " *Of fuch liberty* [or felf-dominion] *as I have now defcribed, it is impoffible that there fhould be an excefs.*" —I, and thefe brave legions, will therefore fight for it, at the hazard of our happinefs and glory. Self-government and fupremacy in hell, are preferable to fervile obedience and fubordinate grandeur in heaven.

I need not tell you, Sir, that this fpeech of the patriotic Seraph is formed upon the principles laid down in Dr. Price's pamphlet. You eafily difcern not only his fentiments, but his very words and doctrine. Should you reply, that the cafe of *creatures* is different from that of fubjects, becaufe *creatures* owe more to *God*, than *fubjects* to an earthly *fovereign :* I grant it, and affert, that on this account obedience to the true God is prefcribed in the *firfl* table of the law, and reafonable fubjection to our rightful fovereign, in the *fecond* table. The former is *the firfl and great commandment. And the fecond is like unto it* in dignity and importance. Therefore fays St. Peter, *Fear God and honour the king.* Give both *God* and *Cæfar* their due. Subject yourfelves to both in their place.

To return : If your doctrine directly or indirectly ftrikes at the authority of *God* and *Cæfar*, as the two preceding fpeeches fhew it does, how dangerous is your patriotifm ! I fhall not however brand it with the epithets which Dr. Price applies to the conduct of his governors, and loyal fellow-fubjects ; nor fhall I borrow from him the words *curfed ambition— madnefs—rage—favage folly,* &c. But with a degree of the liberty, with which Paul *withflood* Peter *to the face becaufe he was to be blamed,* I fhall venture to expoftulate a moment both with him and with you.

You

You are not only *men*, but *Britons, Patriots, Chriſtians*, and *miniſters of the goſpel*. But which of theſe
names do you adorn, when you teach the wretched
politics, which, I truſt, I have refuted in theſe pages ?
If your capital arguments are *irrational*; have you
ſhewn yourſelves *men ?*—If they ſap the foundation of all *civil* government : have you ſhewn yourfelves *civilized* men ?—If they are *unconſtitutional*,
betray Great Britain, tend to rend from her all
her American dominions, and pour undeſerved contempt upon our rightful lawgivers; have you ſhewn
yourſelves *Britons, ſubjects,* and *patriots,* deſervedly
ſo called ?—If they ſubvert an important part of
Chriſt's doctrine, and defeat the effect of his loyal
example; have you ſhewn yourſelves *chriſtians ?*—If
they tend to kindle the fire of national diſcontent,
to make uneaſy ſubjects fly to arms ; or rebellious
ſubjects graſp, with new tranſports of enthuſiaſm,
the ſwords which they wantonly bathe in floods of
Britiſh blood ; have you acted the part of *preachers
of the goſpel of peace ?* Have you ſhewn, that you
either fear God, or honour the king ?—If you have
called all the powers of ſophiſtry and oratory to
your help, to hinder millions of ſubjects from paying obedience to God . by *rendering unto Cæſar the
things which are Cæſar's*; have you not blown the
trumpet of diſcord ? And have you not founded a
falſe alarm thro' the Britiſh dominions, by repreſent-
ing *our conſtitution* as " *almoſt loſt*" thro' the " *weakneſs*" and " *violence*" of our governors, when if there
is any likelihood of its being loſt, the danger ſprings
from the *weakneſs* or *violence* of the patriots, whom
your publications intoxicate and " *kindle into rage ?*"
And ſhall I praiſe you for ſuch a conduct ? No :
Whoever they are, that admire you as bold, ſpirited
citizens, I ſhall take the liberty to conſider you as
raſh injudicious patriots, who have more wit than
prudence, and intend far better than you perform.
    Should you ſay, that you have the approbation
of the minority in parliament, and of the patriots

in the city of London : I reply, that the city-patriots will not be your comforters on your death-bed,
or your judges in the great day. And what if the
majority of mankind were on your fide; could they
caufe a doctrine, which is *irrational, unfcriptural,*
and *unconflitutional,* to be agreeable to reafon, fcripture, and the conftitution ? Permit me, then, my
dear, miftaken fellow-labourers in the gofpel, to
befeech you to review our controverfy, to ftudy
chriftian politicks, to drop your prejudices againft
our governors, to embrace *genuine* patriotifm, and to
fecond the efforts of the minifters of ftate and gofpel
minifters, who try to ftem the torrent of political
enthufiafm, which deluges America, and threatens
to overflow Great Britain itfelf. So fhall you undo
the harm, which you have undefignedly done ; and
our revolted fellow-fubjects, inftead of curfing the
day when you confirmed them in their fin, will blefs
you for giving them an antidote as powerful as
the error, which now poifons their minds, and dif-
tracts their country.

Should you wonder, Sir, at my repeated oppofition to your principles, I fhall urge two things
by way of apology for it : (1) Tho' I believe that
you and your Second *mean* well, yet *fome* of your
principles have, I fear, a tendency to raife or fo-
ment a fpirit of difobedience, fedition, and anarchy. And (2) as a minifter of the church of England, I have fubfcribed to the doctrine of the *Homily againft difobedience and wilful rebellion,* which
contains this remarkable ejaculation. ' God of his
' infinite mercy grant unto us, that we may be—
' good, natural, loving, and obedient fubjects ;—
' not only fhewing all obedience ourfelves, but, *as
' many of us as are able, to the utmoft of our power,
' ability, and underftanding,'* [endeavouring] ' to
' ftay and reprefs all rebels and rebellions againft
' God, our gracious prince, and natural country,
' *at every occafion that is offered unto us !* And that
which

' which we *are all able to do*, unlefs we do it, we
' fhall be moft wicked, and moft worthy to feel in
' the end fuch extreme plagues, as God has ever
' poured upon rebels.' I produce this quotation,
not to charge you, Sir, or Dr. Price, with *difobedience, and wilful* rebellion, for I firmly believe you
intend no fuch thing. I only want to remind you,
that, by my fubfcriptions as a minifter, my baptifm
as a chriftian, and my oath of allegiance as a fubject, I am bound, *at the occafion offered me* by your
reply and your quotations, *to do what* I am *able to
do*, in order to rectify your miftakes, and guard my
readers againft what appears to *me* the natural tendency of your principles. And now, Sir, having
cleared my confcience with refpect to you, and the
ingenious Dr. Price, whom you have called to your
affiftance, I quit the thanklefs office of a faithful
reprover, and refuming that of a friendly controvertift, I affure you, that, notwithftanding the difference of our political and religious fentiments, i
am with chriftian fincerity and love,

Rev. Sir,

Your Obedient

Servant in Chrift,

J. F.

POSTSCRIPT.

IN my firft Letter, I have omitted an important
anfwer to your capital argument. You fuppofe, Sir, that the Colonifts are enflaved and robbed, when they are taxed by the king and the parliament, becaufe " *every fhilling which they* [the

members of the Britifh parliament] *take out of the pocket of an American, is fo much faved in their cawn."* To this I objeft the improbability that a Britifh legiflator would fo far demean himfelf, as to fave a dirty fhilling in his purfe, by oppreffive-ly taking one out of an American's pocket.—You reply by infinuating, that I have not fo high an opinion of the honefty of our legiflators as I ex-prefs; and that, if I lent a few thoufands to one of them, I fhould take care not to part with my money without receiving a proper bond. To the anfwer which I have given you, p. 2S, permit me to add that which follows.

Suppofing that a member of parliament would aft a knave's part for the fake of " a few thou-fands" wherewith he could enrich *himfelf*; yet it is abfurd to fuppofe, that he would turn robber, to fhare his booty with near fix millions of people. For if a member of parliament picks an Ameri-can's pocket by taxing him, the fhilling which he takes from the American does not fave a fhilling in his own pocket, as you infinuate: It is only a fhilling faved for Great Britain in general,—that is, for near fix millions of people. I fhall not fay then, What gentleman is there in parliament,—but what felon is there in Newgate, who would think it worth his while to pick an American's' pocket of a fhilling, or even of three millions of fhillings, to fhare the profit of his villainy among fix millions of people? Your grand argument therefore, confidered in this light, wants not only folidity, but even plaufibility; Since it is founded on an abfurd, uncharitable probability, which falls fhort of a rational probability, almoft as much as a fingle unit falls fhort of fix millions.

The preceding obfervation is applicable to your doftrine of liberty. Civil liberty, if we believe you, Sir, and Dr. Price, is one and the fame thing with the power of making our own laws in commcn with our fellow-fubjects. According to this rotion, fuppofing that, to make our own laws, we

re-

repealed all the laws, which have been made in England by former legiflators;—fuppofing that all the fubjects of Great Britain are *free* in your fenfe of the word; that their number is nine millions; and that one has as much right to make laws as another;—fuppofing this, I fay, upon your fcheme it follows, that the degree of *legiflative power*, i. e. of *liberty*, which falls to the fhare of an Englifhman, bears as infignificant a proportion to *the* FULL *power of legiflation*, i. e. to FULL *liberty*, as a fingle voice bears to eight millions, nine hundred and ninety-nine thoufand, nine hundred and ninety-nine voices. If the crown itfelf, and the power annexed to it, were divided into fo many parts, they would be fo little and fo infignificant, that none but fools would think it worth their while to contend an hour about one fuch part of the royal dignity. But this is not all: If the old adage, *Tot capita, tot fenfus*, is true; —if every man has his peculiar turn for legiflation, as well as his peculiar complexion and look;—if no one is free, but fo far as he is governed according to his own legiflative mind;—if nine millions of Britifh fubjects have as much right to make Britifh laws as Dr. Price;—and if the majority are to carry their point againft the minority; there are nine million degrees of probability to one, that Dr. Price, upon his own fcheme, will be forced to give up his own legiflative will; and that the laws made by others fhall prevail againft his own felf-made laws. And is not this a proof, that, after all the ado he makes about liberty, he only leads us to a liberty, which is as far from what he calls compleat liberty, as a fingle unit is far from nine millions? And that he brings us as near the ftate which you are pleafed to call *abject flavery*, as having only one fhare of that part of the legiflative power, which is lodged in the houfe of commons, out of nine millions of fhares, is near to having nothing to do with legiflation at all? If thefe obfervations are juft, is it not e-vident, Sir, that your doctrine of *civil liberty* refts on

E 4   frivolous

frivolous and irrational refinements, as well as your *American patriotism?*

Permit me to make one more remark upon taxation. Page 47, I have quoted you and Dr. Price, who both agree to mention an act of parliament, where " *certain duties, &c. are said to be* GIVEN *and* GRANTED *by the parliament to the king.*" Looking now into your pamphlet, I take notice, that you put the words *given* and *granted* in Italics. Should you do it to infinuate, that the taxes which we pay are *not* a DEBT, but a FREE GIFT from us and our FELLOW-SUBJECTS; permit me, Sir, to answer your indirect argument by observing, that the *legislative* power being chiefly lodged in the *parliament*, as the *executive* power is chiefly lodged in the *king*; the *legislative* power may with propriety GIVE and GRANT to the *executive* power the revenue arising from such and such taxes. All that can therefore be reasonably inferred from the two expressions, on which you seem to lay so much stress, is that the legislative power *gives* and *grants* supplies to the king, as the first commander of the fleet and army. But to conclude from thence, that taxes are not DUE by *the people* to the *legislative* and *protective power*, is as absurd, unscriptural, and unconstitutional, as to conclude, that all the freeholders are *legislators*, that all who have no vote for parliament-men are *slaves*, and that the supreme and governing power is in the hands of the *governed:*—Three dangerous opinions these, which are to your levelling patriotism, what the three heads of *Cerberus* are to that fabulous monster.

LETTER IV.

REV. SIR,

I Should be inexcufeable if I concluded my refutation of Dr. Price's *antichriftian* politicks, without doing him the juftice to confefs, that he has advanced a *chriftian* argument, which I cannot properly anfwer, and which is fo awful, that it highly deferves the attention of all, who wifh well to church and ftate : Take it in his own words.'—" In this hour of tremendous danger, it would become us to turn our thoughts to heaven. This is what our brethren in the Colonies are doing. From one end of North America to the other, they are FASTING and PRAYING. But what are we doing ?—Shocking thought ! we are ridiculing them as *fanatics*, and fcoffing at religion. We are running wild after pleafure, and forgetting every thing ferious and decent at mafquerades. We are gambling in gaming houfes ; trafficking for boroughs ; perjuring ourfelves at elections ; and felling ourfelves for places. Which fide then is Providence likely to favour ? In *America* we fee a number of rifing ftates in the vigour of youth, &c. and animated by PIETY. Here we fee an old ftate, &c. inflated and IRRELIGIOUS, enervated by luxury, &c. and hanging by a thread. Can we look without pain on the iffue ?"

E 5

There

There is more folidity in this argument, than
in all that Dr. Price has advanced. If the Colonifts throng the houfes of God, while we throng
play-houfes, or houfes of ill fame ; if they croud
their communion-tables, while we croud the gaming table or the feftal board ; if they pray, while
we curfe ; if they faft, while we get drunk ; and
keep the fabbath, while we pollute it ; if they
fhelter under the protection of heaven, while our
chief attention is turned to our hired troops ; we are
in danger—in *great* danger. Be our caufe ever fo
good, and our force ever fo formidable ; our cafe
is bad, and our fuccefs doubtful. Nay, *the Lord
of hofts*, who, of old, fold his difobedient people
into the hands of their unrighteous enemies, to
chaftife and humble them,—this righteous Lord,
may give fuccefs to the arms of the Colonies, to
punifh *them* for their revolt, and *us* for our prophanenefs. A youth that believes and prays as
David, is a match for a giant that fwaggers and
curfes as Goliath. And they that, in the name of
the Lord, *enthufiaftically* encounter their enemies in
a *bad* caufe, bid fairer for fuccefs than they that,
in a *good* caufe, *prophanely* go into the field ; truft-
ing only in the apparent ftrength of an arm of
flefh. To difregard the *king's* righteous commands,
as the Colonifts do, is bad : But to defpife the firft-
table commandments of the *King of kings*, as we do,
is ftill worfe. Nor do I fee how we can anfwer it,
either to reafon or our own confciences, to be fo *intent* on inforcing Britifh laws, and fo *remifs* in yield-
ing obedience to the laws of God. If the capital
command, *Fear God, and honour the king*, could be
properly parted ; fhould not every chriftian prefer
the former part to the later ? Will our honouring
the *king* atone for our difhonouring *God* ? And can
we expect, that our loyalty fhall make amends for
our impiety or lukewarmnefs ?

Is it not furprizing, that amidft all the prepara-
tions, which have been made to fubdue the revolted
Colonies, none fhould have been made to check

our

our open rebellion againſt God ; and that in all
our national applications to foreign princes for
help, we ſhould have forgotten a public application to *the Prince of the kings of the earth ?* Many
well-wiſhers to their country flattered themſelves,
that at a time, when the Britiſh empire ſtands, as
Dr. Price juſtly obſerves, " on an edge ſo perilous," our ſuperiors would have appointed a day of
humiliation and prayer ;—a day to confeſs the national ſins, which have provoked God to let looſe a
ſpirit of political enthuſiaſm and revolt upon us ;—a
day to implore pardon for our paſt tranſgreſſions,
and to reſolve upon a more religious and loyal
courſe of life ;—a day to beſeech the Father of
lights and mercies to *teach* at this important juncture, *our ſenators wiſdom* in a peculiar manner ; and
to inſpire them with ſuch ſteadineſs and mildneſs,
that by their prudence, courage, and condeſcention,
the war may be ended with little effuſion of blood ;
and, if poſſible, without ſhedding any more blood
at all.—Thouſands expected to ſee ſuch a day ;
thinking that it becomes us, as reformed chriſtians, nationally to addreſs the throne of grace, and
intreat God to turn the hearts of the Coloniſts towards us, and ours towards them, that we may
ſpeedily bury our mutual animoſities in the grave
of our common Saviour. And not a few ſuppoſed,
that humanity bids us feel for the myriads of our
fellow-creatures, who are going to offer up their
lives in the field of battle ; and that charity and
piety require us to pray that they may penitently
part with their ſins, and ſolemnly prepare themſelves for a ſafe paſſage, I ſhall not ſay from Britain
to America ; but, if they are called to it, from
time into eternity.—Such, I ſay were the expecta-
tions of thouſands, but hitherto their hopes and
wiſhes have been diſappointed.

Dr. Price knows how to avail himſelf of our
omiſſion or delay in this reſpect, to ſtrengthen the
hands of the American patriots, by inſinuating,

that heaven will not be propitious to us ; and that " *our cause is such, as gives us* [no] *reason to ask God to bless it.*" None can tell what fewel this plaufible obfervation of his, will add to the wild fire of political enthufiafm, which burns already too fiercely in the breafts of thoufands of injudicious religionifts. I therefore humbly hope, that our governors will confider Dr. Price's objection taken from our immorality and prophanenefs ; and that they will let the world fee, we are neither afhamed nor afraid to fpread the juftice of our caufe before the Lord of hofts, and to implore his blefling upon the army going to America, to enforce gracious offers of mercy, and reafonable terms of reconciliation.

And why, after all, fhould we be afhamed of afking help of *God*, as well as of German princes ? Have we never read fuch awful fcriptures as thefe ? ' Save us, O king of heaven, WHEN we call upon ' THEE. Some put their truft in chariots, and ' fome in horfes : But WE WILL remember the ' name of the Lord our God.—Bleffed be my ftrong ' helper, who SUBDUETH the people unto me, ' and fetteth me above mine adverfaries.—Thro' ' THEE will we overthrow our enemies, and in THY ' name will we tread them under that rife againft ' us. For I will not truft in my bow : It is not my - ' fword that fhall [*comparatively*] help me.—Be not ' afraid of this * great multitude ; for the battle is ' not yours, but God's.—All the affembly fhall ' know, that the Lord faveth not with fword and ' fpear : For the battle is the LORD's.'

Our own hiftory, as well as the fcripture, confirms Dr. Price's objection taken from our neglect

of

* Dr. Price, fpeaking of the numbers of the Americans, fays,
" To think of conquering that whole continent with 30,000 or
" 40,000 men, to be tranfported acrofs the Atlantic, and fed
" from hence, and incapable of being recruited after any defeat
" —This is folly fo great, that language does not afford a name
" for it."

of the *religious* means of fuccefs in the prefent conteſt. It is well known to many, that in the civil
wars of the laſt age, a national difregard of the
Lord's day, and the avowed contempt of God's
name, which prevailed in the king's party, did
him unfpeakable injury. For multitudes of men
who feared God, feeing prophanenefs reign in the
army of the royaliſts, while religious duty was fo-
lemnly performed by the forces of the parliament;
and being unable to enter into the political quef-
tions, whence the quarrel aroſe, judged of the cauſe
according to religious appearances; and fided
againſt the king, merely becauſe they fancied that
he fided againſt God. Nor were there wanting men
of the greateſt candour and penetration, who
thought, that this was one of the principle cauſes
of the overthrow of our church and ſtate; Cromwell *then* availing himfelf of this appearance, as
Dr. Price does *now*, to perfuade *religious* people,
that he was fighting the Lord's battles, and that
oppoſing the king and the biſhops, was only oppoſing tyranny and a prophane *hierarchy*.   To
ſhew how much our want of religious decency
contributed towards the overthrow of our church
and government in the laſt century, I ſhall produce an other extract from the *Rev. Mr. Baxter's
Narrative of his life and times.* That candid divine
and judicious politician, after mentioning the unhappy differences between thoſe who conform to
the church of England, and thoſe who do not,
ſays:
     Page 32, &c. ' When they [the nonconformiſts]
' had been a while called by that name, [*Puritans*]
' the vicious multitude of the ungodly called all
' *Puritans*, that were ſtrict and ferious, were they
' ever fo conformable: So that the fame name, in
' a Biſhop's mouth, fignified a *Nonconformiſt*; and
' in an ignorant drunkard's or fwearer's mouth,
' fignified a *godly chriſtian*. But the people, being
' the greater number, became among themſelves
                                   ' maſters

' matters of the fenfe.—The ignorant rabble hear-
' ing that the bifhops were againft the *Puritans*
' [not having wit to know whom they meant] were
' emboldened the more againft all thofe whom
' THEY called *Puritans* themfelves; their rage
' againft the *godly* was encreafed; and they cried
' up the bifhops, &c. becaufe they were againft
' the *Puritans.*—Thus the interefts of the Diocef-
' ans, and of the prophane fort of people, were·
' unhappily twifted.'

' As all the Nonconformifts were againft the
' prelates,' [*whofe interefl was clofely connected with*
the king's] ' fo others of the moft *godly* people
' were alienated from the bifhops; becaufe the
' malignant fort were permitted to make *religious*
' perfons their common fcorn;—becaufe they faw
' fo many vicious men among the conformable
' clergy;—becaufe *fafting* and *praying*, &c, were
' fo ftrictly looked after, that the bifhop's courts
' did make it much more perilous, than common
' fwearing and drunkennefs proved to the ungod-
' ly;—becaufe the book, that was publifhed for
' *Recreations on the Lord's day*, made them think,
' that the bifhops concurred with the prophane;.
' —becaufe fo great a number of conformable mi-
' nifters were fufpended or punifhed for not read-
' ing the *Book of fports on Sundays*,. &c. and fo
' many thoufand families, and many worthy mi-
' nifters driven out of the land, &c.—all thefe,
' upon my own knowledge, were the true caufes,
' why fo great a number of thofe perfons, who
' were counted *moft religious*, fell in with the par-
' liament; infomuch that the generality of the
' ftricter fort of preachers joined with them.—
' Very few of all that learned and pious fynod at
' Weftminfter were Nonconformifts before, and
' yet were for the parliament; fuppofing that the
' intereft of *religion* lay on that fide.'—

' Upon my knowledge, many that were not wife
' enough to underftand the truth about the caufe
' of the king and parliament, did yet run into the
· parliament's

' parliament's armies, or take their part, as sheep
' do together for Company; being moved by this
' argument, " Sure God will not suffer almost all
'' his most *religious* servants to err in so great a
'' matter: If these should perish, what will be-
'' come of *religion ?*"—' But these were insuffi-
' cient grounds to go upon. And abundance of
' the ignorant sort of the country, who were ci-
' vil, did flock in to the parliament, and filled
' up their armies afterwards, merely because they
' heard men *swear* for the common prayers and
' bishops, and heard others *pray* that were against
' them ; and because they heard the king's sol-
' diers with horrid oaths abuse the name of God,
' and saw them live in debauchery ; and the par-
' liament's soldiers flock to sermons, talk of reli-
' gion, and pray and sing psalms together on
' their guards. All the sober men, that I was ac-
' quainted with, who were against the parliament,
' were wont to say : The king has *the better*
' CAUSE, but the parliament has *the better* MEN.
' And indeed this unhappy complication of the
' interest of prelacy and prophaneness, and this
' opposition of the interest of prelacy to the tem-
' per of the generality of the *religious* party, was
' the VISIBLE CAUSE of the overthrow of the
' king, in the eye of all the understanding world.'
    Page 31. ' Though it must be confessed, that the
' public safety, and liberty wrought very much
', with most, especially the nobility and gentry,
' who adhered to the parliament: Yet was it
' PRINCIPALLY the differences about *religious*
' matters, that filled up the parliament's armies,
' and put into their soldiers the RESOLUTION and
' VALOUR, which carried them on in another
' manner than mercenary soldiers are carried on.
' Not that the matter of *bishops* or *no bishops*
' was the main thing ; though many called it *bel-*
' *lum episcopale* : For thousands that wished for
' *good bishops* were on the parliament's side.
' But the *generality* of the people [I say not
' *all*] who used to talk of God and heaven,
                                              ' and

‘ and fcripture and holinefs, and read books of
‘ devotion, and pray in their families, and fpend
‘ the Lord's day in religious exercifes, and fpeak
‘ againft fwearing, curfing, drunkennefs, prophane-
‘ nefs, &c. I fay, the main body of this fort of
‘ men adhered to the parliament. And on the
‘ other fide, the gentry that were not fo precife and
‘ ftrict againft an oath, or gaming, or plays, or
‘ drinking; nor troubled themfelves fo much about
‘ God and the world to come ; and the miniﬅers
‘ and people that were for the king's *Book for danc-*
‘ *ing and recreation on the Lord's days* ; and thofe that
‘ made no fo great a matter of every fin, but were
‘ glad to hear a fermon which lafhed the *Puritans,*
‘ &c. the main body of thefe were againft the par-
‘ liament.’

Page 44. ‘ And here I muft repeat the GREAT
‘ CAUSE of the parliament's ftrength, and the
‘ KING'S RUIN : and that was, that the debauched
‘ rabble thro’ the land, emboldened by his gentry,
‘ and feconded by the common foldiers of his ar-
‘ my, took all that were called *Puritans* for their
‘ enemies. And tho’ fome of the king's gentry
‘ and fuperior officers were fo civil, that they
‘ would do no fuch thing; yet that was no fecu-
‘ rity to the country, while the multitude did what
‘ they lift. So that if any one was noted for a
‘ ftrict preacher, or for a man of a pious life, he
‘ was plundered or abufe, and in danger of his
‘ life. And if a man did but pray in his family,
‘ or were but heard to repeat a fermon, or fing a
‘ pfalm, they cried out *Rebels ! Round-heads!* and
‘ all their goods that were portable proved guilty,
‘ how innocent foever they were themfelves. I.
‘ fuppofe this was kept from the knowledge of the
‘ king, and perhaps of many fober Lords of the
‘ council ; for few could come near them ; and it
‘ is the fate of fuch, not to believe *evil* of thofe
‘ that they think are *for* them ; nor *good* of thofe
‘ that they think are *againﬅ* them. But, upon my
‘ certain knowledge, this was it that filled the ar-
‘ mies

' mies and garrifons of the parliament with *fober*
' *pious* men. Thoufands had no mind to meddle
' with the wars, but greatly defired to live peace-
' ably at home, when the rage of foldiers and
' drunkards would not let them. Some ftayed till
' they had been plundered, perhaps twice or thrice
' over,—but moft were afraid of their lives, and oft
' they fought refuge in the parliament's garrifons,—
' and were fain to take up arms and be foldiers to
' get bread.'
   Mr. Baxter's account of Cromwell's charaɛter,
and of his *religious* troop, is too remarkable not to
deferve a place in this extraɛt. P. 98, ' No mere
' man was *better* and *worfe* fpoken of than he
' Cromwell], ' according as men's interefts led their
' judgments. The foldiers and feɛtaries moft highly
' magnified him, till he began to feek the crown.
' And then there were fo many that would be *half-*
' *kings* themfelves, that a *king* did feem intolerable
' to them. The royalifts abhorred him as a moft
' perfidious hypocrite; and the Prefbyterians
' thought him little better. If, after fo many
' others, I may fpeak my opinion of him, I think,
' that having been a prodigal in his youth, and
' afterwards changed into a *zealous religionift*, he
' meant honeftly in the main courfe of his life, *till*
' profperity and fuccefs corrupted him. At his firft
' entrance into the wars, being but a captain of
' horfe, he had fpecial care to get *religious* men
' into his troop. Thefe men were of greater un-
' derftanding than common foldiers, and therefore
' were more apprehenfive of the importance of
' the war; and making not money, but that which
' *they* took for the public felicity, to be their end,
' they were the more engaged to be valiant. For
' he, that makes money his end, efteems his life
' above his pay, and therefore is likely enough to
' fave it by flight, when danger comes. But he,
' that maketh the felicity of church and ftate his
' end, efteemeth it above his life, and therefore
' will the fooner lay down his life for it.—This
                                              ' Cromwel

' Cromwell underflood, and that none would be
' fuch valiant men as the *religious*. I conjecture,
' that, at his firft chufing fuch men into his troop,
' it was the very efteem and love of *religious* men
' that principally moved him. By this means, he
' fped better than he expected. That troop did
' prove fo valiant, that, as far as I could learn,
' they never once ran away before an enemy.
' Hereupon he got a commiffion, and brought
' this troop into a double regiment of fourteen
' full troops; and all thefe as full of *religious* men
' as he could get. Thefe having more than or-
' dinary wit and refolution, had more than ordi-
' nary fuccefs. With their fucceffes, the hearts
' both of captain and foldiers fecretly rofe both in
' pride and expectation; and the familiarity of ma-
' ny honeft, erroneous men, Anabaptifts, Anti-
' nomians, &c. began withal quickly to corrupt
' their judgments. Hereupon Cromwell's *religious*
' zeal giveth way to the power of that ambition,
' which ftill increafeth as his fucceffes increafe.
' Both *piety* and *ambition* concurred in his counte-
' nancing all that he thought *godly*. Piety plead-
' eth for them as *godly*, and ambition fecretly tell-
' eth him what ufe he might make of them. He
' meaneth well in all this at the beginning, and
' thinketh that he does all for the fafety of the
' *godly*, and the public good; but not without an
' eye to himfelf*.'

From

---

* No hiftorian having had fo good an opportunity of knowing
Cromwell, as judicious Mr. Baxter, who was perfonally acquainted with him, and ferved in his army as chaplain; fome
of my readers will be glad to fee, what he further fays of that
extraordinary man.

' When fucceffes had broken down all confiderable oppofition,
' he [Cromwell] was in the face of the ftrongeft temptations,
' which conquered him, when he had conquered others. He
' thought that he had hitherto done well; that none but God had
' made him great; that if the war was lawful, the victory was
' lawful; that if it was lawful to fight againft the king and con-
' quer.

From this extract it appears, that Cromwell, like Dr. Price, rode the great horfe *Religion*, as well as the great horfe *Liberty*; and that the beſt way to counter-work the enthufiaſm of patriotic religioniſts, is to do conſtitutional *Liberty* and ſcriptural *Religion* FULL JUSTICE; by defending the *former* againſt the attacks of *defpotic monarchs* on the right hand, and *defpotic mobs* on the left; and by preſerving the *latter* from the oppoſite onſets of *prophane infidels* on the left hand, and *enthufiaſtical religioniſts* on the right. I humbly hope, that our governors will always ſo avoid one extreme, as not to run into the other; and that, at this time, they will ſo guard againſt the very appearances of irreligion and immorality, as to leave Dr. Price, ſo far

as

'quer him, it was lawful to uſe him as a conquered enemy; and
'that it would be a fooliſh thing to truſt him, when they had ſo
'provoked him. Hereupon he joined with that party in the par-
'liament, who were for cutting off the king, and raiſed with
'them the independents and ſectaries in the army, city, and
'country, to make a faction. Accordingly he modelled the army,
'diſbanded the forces which were like to have hindered his de-
'fign, pulled down the preſbyterian majority in parliament—and
'then the parliament; being the more eaſily perſuaded that all
'this was lawful, becauſe he had a ſecret eye to his own exalta-
'tion; thinking that when the king was gone, a government
'there muſt be, and that no man was ſo fit for it as himſelf—
'Having thus forced his conſcience to juſtify *all* his cauſe, he
'thinketh that the end being good and neceſſary, the neceſſary
'means cannot be bad. And accordingly, he giveth his intereſt
'leave to tell him, how far promiſes and vows ſhall be kept or
'broken.—Hence he thought ſecrecy a virtue, diſſimulating no
'vice, and a lie, or perfidiouſneſs tolerable in caſe of neceſſity.—
'His name ſtandeth as a monitory monument to poſterity, to tell
'them the *inſtability* of man in ſtrong temptations;—what *great
'ſucceſs* can do to *lift up* the mind;—what *pride* can do to make
'man *ſelfiſh*;—what *ſelfiſhneſs* can do to bribe the conſcience,
'corrupt the judgment, and make men juſtify the greateſt ſins;—
'and what bloodſhed and great enormities a deluded judgment
'may draw men into.'—Hence it appears, candid Mr. Baxter
believed, that Cromwell was once a good and pious man, who
fell from God's fear into complicated wickedneſs, thro' the external allurements of *ſucceſs* and *ambition*, and thro' the internal
ſnare of *antinomianiſm*.

as in them lies, no room to injure our caufe by arguments taken from our want of devotion and of a
ſtrict regard to found morals. What we owe to
God, to ourſelves, and to the Coloniſts, calls upon
us to remove whatever may give any juſt offence to
thoſe who feek occaſion to reflect upon us. The
Coloniſts narrowly watch us : Let their keen in-
ſpection make us diligently watch ourſelves.

Let us eſpecially take care neither to embezzle,
nor miſapply the national income : But, as faithful guardians and ſtewards of the money raiſed for
the neceſſary expences of the government, let us
[as many as are entruſted with the collecting or
expending of that conſecrated treaſure] ſhew ourfelves diſintereſted, thrifty, and invariably juſt.
Nothing can render our doctrine of taxation odious
to conſcientious people, but a needleſs rigor in the
collecting, and a wanton profuſion in the ſpending
of the public revenue. I know that uneaſy men,
intent upon ſedition and revolt, are apt to ſay
whatever can palliate their crime. The leaſt miſ-
demeanor of individuals, let it be ever fo much
hid from, or diſapproved of by our governors,
will always appear to ſuch men a ſufficient reaſon
to pour floods of reproach upon the adminiſtration.
Thus, if we may depend upon the *St. James's Chro-
nicle*‘ " Dr. *Franklin*, a member of the American
" Congreſs," inſinuates, that " the government
" is made deteſtable by governors, who when they
" have crammed their coffers, and made them-
" felves fo odious to the people, that they can no
" longer remain among them with ſafety to their
" perſons, are recalled and rewarded with pen-
" ſions :—That the produce of the taxes is not
" applied to the defence of the provinces, and
" the better ſupport of government ; but beſtow-
" ed where it is not neceſſary, in augmenting ſa-
" laries, or penſions :—And that a board of offi-
" cers compoſed of the moſt indiſcreet, illbred,
" and inſolent men that can be found, live in
" open, grating luxury upon the ſweat and blood
" of

" of the induſtrious, whom they worry with ground-
" leſs and expenſive proſecutions, before arbitrary
" revenue-judges."—I hope, for the honour of the
adminiſtration, that prejudice guided Dr. Franklin's pen, when it dropped theſe invidious hints.
Should we have given them any juſt ground of
complaint, it becomes us to remove it with all ſpeed:
ſetting our ſeal to the noble maxim, which Dr.
Price advances after Lord Chatham; *Rectitude is
dignity. Oppreſſion only is meanneſs; and juſtice,
honour.*

Righteouſneſs exalteth a nation, ſays the wiſe man,
but ſin is a reproach to any people, and may prove
the ruin of the moſt powerful empire. Violence
brought on the deluge. Luxury overthrew Sodom.
Cruel uſage of the Iſraelites deſtroyed Egypt.
Complete wickedneſs cauſed the extirpation of the
Canaanites. Imperiouſneſs, and an abuſe of the
power of taxation, rent ten tribes from the kingdom of Judah. Pride ſunk Babylon. Nineveh
and Jeruſalem, by timely repentance, once rever-
ſed their awful doom; but returning to their former ſins, they ſhared at laſt the fate of all the ſtates,
which have *filled up the meaſure of their iniquities.*—
And have we taken ſo few ſtrides towards that awful period, as to render national repentance needleſs in this day of trouble? By fomenting contentions and wars among the natives of Africa, in
order to buy the priſoners whom they take from
each other; have not ſome of our countrymen
turned Africa into a field of blood? Do not the
ſighs of myriads of innocent negroes unjuſtly
tranſported from their native country to the Britiſh
dominions, call night and day for vengeance upon
us; whilſt their groans upbraid the hypocritical
friends of liberty, who buy, and ſell, and whip
their fellow men as if they were brutes; and ab-
ſurdly complain that *they* are enſlaved, when it is
they themſelves, who deal in the liberties and bodies of men, as graziers do in the liberties and bodies of oxen?

And

And is what I beg leave to call our *Nabob-trade*
in the *Eaſt*, more conſiſtent with humanity, than
our *ſlave-trade* in the *South* and *Weſt?* Who can
tell how many myriads of men have been cut off
in the Eaſt Indies by famine or wars, which had
their riſe from the ambition, covetouſneſs, and
cruelty of ſome of our countrymen? And if no
vindictive notice has been taken of theſe barbarous
and bloody ſcenes, has not the nation made them
in ſome degree her own? And does not that innocent blood, the price of which has been imported with impunity, and now circulates through
the kingdom to feed our luxury—does not all that
blood, I ſay, ſpeak louder for vengeance againſt
us, than the blood of Abel did againſt his murder-
ous brother?—" The juſtice of the nation, ſays
Dr. Price, has ſlept over theſe enormities: Will
the juſtice of heaven ſleep?"—No: but it ſtill patiently waits for our reformation; nor will it, I
hope, wait in vain; but if it does, the ſuſpended
blow will in the end deſcend with redoubled force,
and ſtrike us with aggravated ruin. For God will
be avenged on all impenitent nations: He has one
rule for them and for individuals: *Except* they *re-
pent*, ſays Chriſt himſelf, they *ſhall all likewiſe
periſh*.

Let our *devotion* be improved by the American
controverſy, as well as our *morals*. Inſtead of
" *ſcoffing at religion*," as Dr. Price ſays we do, let
us honour the piety of the Coloniſts. So far at
leaſt, as their religious profeſſions are conſiſtent,
ſincere, and ſcriptural, let them provoke us to a
rational concern for the glory of God, and our eternal intereſts. Were we to contend with our American Colonies for *ſupremacy* in VIRTUE and DEVO-
TION, how noble would be the ſtrife! How worthy
of a proteſtant kingdom, and a mother-country!
And does not political wiſdom, as well as brotherly
love, require us to do ſomething in order to root
up their inveterate prejudices againſt us and our
church? Have we forgotten that many of the firſt
Coloniſts

Colonifts croffed the Atlantic for confcience' fake ;
feeking in the woods of America, fome, a fhelter
againft our once perfecuting hierarchy ; and others,
a refuge from our epidemical prophanenefs ? And
does not their offspring look upon us in the fame
odious light, in which Dr. Price places us ? Do
they not abhor or defpife us, as impious, immoral
men, " *enervated by luxury* ; "—men, with whom
it is dangerous to be connected, and who " *may*
" *expect calamities, that fhall recover to reflection*"
[*perhaps to* DEVOTION] " *Libertines and Atheifts*"
themfelves ?

And is it only for God's fake, for the fake
of our own fouls, and for the fake of the Colonifts,
that we fhould look to our conduct and chriftian
profeffion ? Are there not multitudes of rafh religionifts in the kingdom, who fuppofe that all the
praying people in England are for the Americans,
and who warmly efpoufe their part, merely becaufe
they are told, that the Colonifts " *faft and pray*,"
while " *we forget every thing ferious and decent*,"
and becaufe prejudiced teachers confidently afk,
with Dr. Price, " *Which fide is providence likely to
favour* ?"—Would to God all our legiflators felt
the weight of this objection, which can as eafily
miflead moral and religious people in the prefent
age, as it did in the laft ! Would to God they exerted themfelves in fuch a manner, that all unprejudiced men might fee, the king and parliament
have " the better men," as well as " the better
caufe !" Would to God, that by timely reformation, and folemn addreffes to the throne of grace,
we might convince Dr. Price and all the Americans, that in fubmitting to the Britifh legiflature,
they will not fubmit to *libertinifm* and *atheifm* ;
but to a venerable body of virtuous and godly fenators, who know that the firft care of *God's* reprefentatives on earth—the principal ftudy of political *gods*, fhould be to promote God's fear, by
fetting a good example before the people committed

ted to their charge, and by steadily enforcing the observance of the moral law !'

I need not tell you, Sir, what effect this would have upon our pious American brethren. You feel it in your own breast. The bare idea of such a reformation softens your prejudices. Were it to take place, it would overcome Dr. Price himself. Pious joy would set him upon writing as warmly for the government, as he has done against it; and in the midst of his deep repentance for the dangerous errors he has published, he would have the consolation to think, that one of his *observations* has done more good, than all his sophisms have done mischief. These are some of the reflections, which Dr. Price's *religious* argument has drawn from my pen, and which I doubt not but some of our Governors have already made by the help of that wisdom, which prompts them to improve our former calamities, and to study what may promote our happiness in church and state.'

I am, &c.

LETTER V.

REV. SIR,

CHRISTIANS are, in a special manner, debtors to all mankind. I owe love to all my fellow-subjects, as well as loyalty to the king, and duty to the parliament: and my love to our American Colonies, as well as my regard for equity, obliges me to say what can *reasonably* be said on their behalf; that prejudice, on both sides, may give place to christian forbearance and conciliatory kindness.

I hope, Sir, you are, by this time, convinced that the American revolt is absolutely unjustifiable; and that the king and parliament have an indubitable right *proportionably* to tax the Colonists, as well as the English; although the Colonists are not *directly* and *adequately* represented in parliament, any more than multitudes of Britons who live abroad, and millions who reside in Great Britain. And now, Sir, I candidly allow, that, although the Colonists cannot without absurdity insist on an *equal* representation, yet they may humbly request to be particularly represented in the British legislature: and that, altho' strict justice does not oblige Great Britain to grant them such a request; yet parental wisdom, and brotherly condescension, require her to grant something to the notion, that a *direct* representation in parliament is inseparably connected with civil liberty. This notion, I confess, is irrational, unscriptural, and unconstitutional: But it

F   is

is a prevailing notion ; and if we look at it in one
point of view, it seems to wear the badge of *British*
liberty, and therefore has some claim to the indulgence of Britons.

Permit me to illustrate my meaning by a scriptural simile. Thro' a strong national prejudice, the
Jews who had embraced christianity fancied, that
no man could be a true christian without being
circumcised ; and they supported their assertion
by God's positive command to the Father of the
faithful,—a command this, which Christ had not
expressly repealed, and to which he and his disci-
ples had religiously submitted. The apostles saw
that the christianized Jews were under a capital
mistake. Nevertheless [in condescension to human
weakness and national prejudice] they allowed
them to circumcise their children ; and Paul himself, tho' he detested their error, yielded to them
so far as to have his convert Timothy circumcised.
I grant that a *direct* and *adequate* representation in
parliament is no more essential to British liberty,
than circumcision to true christianity. But, as the
governors of the christian church made some concessions to Jewish weakness ; might not also the
governors of the British empire make some to American prejudice ; especially considering, that it will
be as difficult for them peaceably to rule the Americans without such an act of condescension ; as it
would have been for the apostles to govern the Jews,
without the above mentioned complaisance ?

Besides, in some cases, constitutional and unconstitutional taxation may border so nearly upon each
other, that the most judicious politicians will be as
much at a loss to draw the line between them, as
the most skillful painter would be to draw the line
between the primitive colours of the rainbow. This
bordering of a faint constitutional privilege, upon
an unconstitutional, absolute want of privilege, has
deceived the Colonists. As a man, who is passio-
nately fond of flaming crimson, takes a faint red to
be no red at all ; they have pronounced that to be
                                                no

no reprefentation, which is an *indirect* reprefentation difcernible to all but the prejudiced. In their patriotic fright they have fancied that the fhip of conftitutional liberty ftruck on a rock, becaufe it did not carry fo many fails as they imagined it fhould. You may compare their miftake to that of impatient fufpicious paffengers, who, when they have all their fortune with them on board a fhip, are apt to think, that fhe does not move at all, be-caufe her motion is not fo rapid as they could wifh; and becaufe their anxious fears turn every fail they fee, into a privateer in chafe of their property. Their error deferves then compaffion, as well as blame; and will appear exculable to thofe who know the immenfe value of *liberty*.

Our lawgivers, who are peculiarly acquainted with the worth of this jewel, can above all men put a favourable conftruction upon the panick of a peo-ple afraid of being enflaved. Depending therefore on their condefcenfion, I fhall prefume to afk, if now, that the government has plainly afferted, and powerfully fupported the *juft* claims of Great Bri-tain, it might not fafely relax a little the reins of authority, and kindly condefcend to the fears of the Colonifts. And fhould the Americans fhew themfelves *juft* in indemnifying our injured mer-chants, *penitent* in laying down their arms, and *loyal* in acknowledging the right, that Great Britain has to expect proportionable taxes from them: might not the king and parliament fhew themfelves *kind*, in granting them the privilege of a *fpecial* reprefen-tation in the Britifh legiflature; or in paffing an *act of fecurity*, to fix juft bounds to the power of parliamentary taxation with refpect to the Ameri-cans;—to promife the Colonies, that a proper al-lowance fhall always be made them for the fuperior commercial privileges of Great Britain;—to afcer-tain, in an equitable manner, the quantum of that allowance;—and to remove their dread of being dif-proportionably taxed, by the moft folemn affuran-ces, that their taxes fhall always rife or fall in exact proportion to our own, according to the plan laid down in p. 51?

I would not carry matters so far as to say, with the poet, *Summum jus summa injuria** ; but might I not observe that parental love, brotherly kindness, and British equity require, that some condescension be shewn to the Colonists? Should not British legislators shew themselves *gods*, by imitating the God *of Gods*,

> Who conquers all, beneath, above,
> Devils with force, and men with *love*?

Whilst the Atlantic foams under the weight of the transports, which carry the troops sent over to subdue the revolted provinces, might not love suspend the destructive stroke, and conquer them without farther effusion of blood? Is their hardness absolutely desperate? Whilst the sight of a force so superior to that, which quelled them at *Bunker's Hill*, works upon their prudence; and whilst scriptural expostulations enlighten their consciences; might not some gracious and timely concessions work upon their gratitude, excite their admiration, and regain their confidence? O that you, Sir, and I could imitate those courageous women, who when the Romans their husbands, and the Sabines their brothers, were going to engage, rushed between the two armies, and so wrought upon them by tender expostulations, that the fierce antagonists, instead of plunging their swords into each others' breasts, fell upon each others' necks, and turned the field of *battle* into a field of *reconciliation!* If an heathen country saw the delightful scene, might not a christian land behold it also?— The pleasing thought transports my mind:—My imagination warmed by the fond hope carries me beyond myself:—Methinks I rush between the parliament

---

* *Right carried to the height, is the height of injustice.*

liament and the Congrefs, and after having pleaded
the fovereign's caufe before the patriots, I plead that
of the patriots before the fovereign. Fancying myfelf at the foot of the throne, and feeing the King
raifed on high above all the Britifh lawgivers, on my
bended knees, from the duft, with trembling awe,
I prefent my bold, mediatorial plea.

O KING, live and reign in righteoufnefs for
ever! And ye, his Patrician and ‡ Plebeian fenators, help him long to fway the fceptre with chriftian gentlenefs and Britifh fortitude! As his faithful
affeffors, and partakers with him of the legiflative
power, firmly fupport on his royal head the ponderous crown, which gives him the dominion over
the Britifh iflands, half of the weftern world, and
the whole aqueous globe!—One of your adopted
fubjects, warmed with gratitude for the religious
and civil liberty, which he enjoys under your mild
government; and deeply concerned for your glory
and the profperity of your dominions, intrudes into

F 3   your

---

‡ There is a fymmetrical excellence in the Britifh conftitution,
which efcapes the attention of many Britons. I have obferved,
that the capital bufinefs of the parliament is to keep the balance
even between the king and the people; that neither oppreffive
defpotifm, [or the tyrranny of one,] nor mobbing anarchy, [or
the tyrrany of many,] may prevail. I now add, that the two
houfes of parliament are two *mediatorial* courts between the king
and the people. The houfe of *commons* is compofed of fenators
chofen by the *people* to be a check upon the king and his nobles;
and the houfe of *lords* is compofed of fenators chofen by the *kings*,
to be a check upon the people and their reprefentatives. Hence
it appears, that the houfe of lords is peculiarly bound to maintain
the prerogatives of the crown, againft the encroachments of mobs
and mobbing pa riots; and that it is the peculiar duty of the houfe
of commons to maintain the privileges of the people, againft the
incroachments of defpots and defpotic minifters. In the laft century the lords failing in their duty, the balance was broken: The
commons prevailed; and the confequence was what might naturally be expected: The houfe of lords was fet afide, the king beheaded, and the conftitution overthrown. This remarkable e-
vent fhould teach our fenators the wifdom peculiarly neceffary to
a faithful difcharge of their high office.

your awful prefence to intercede for his guilty brethren. If the KING of kings, and LORD of lords,
vouchſafes to receive his fervent addreſſes to the
throne of grace for you; do not rejeƈt, O ye gods,
his humble addreſs for your American Colonies.

It is not my defign to extenuate their crime. An
ingenuous confeſſion becomes a proſtrate ſupplicant.
—They have finned againſt heaven and againſt you.
—They have prepoſterouſly charged *you* with robbery, when it was they themſelves who robbed * *God*,
by keeping from his political repreſentatives, the
refonable and legal taxes *due* to the ſupreme power;
—to a creative and proteƈtive power that gave them
birth, and raiſed them from a ſtate of infant weakneſs and want, to youthful vigor and growing opu-
lence. Their crime is complicate: They have
openly encouraged the lawleſs mobs, which tramp-
led upon your authority, and deſtroyed the property
of your loyal ſubjeƈts:—They have obſtinately pro-
teƈted felony and ſedition:— They have audaci-
ouſly hindered the courſe of juſtice:—Their Congreſs has met to oppofe your claim of taxation in
the capital of that very province, by the *expreſs
terms* of whoſe CHARTER they are ſolemnly bound
to pay you taxes.—They have armed by ſea and land
to cut off your forces:—And, not ſatisfied with
aſſerting their aſſumed ſupremacy over the revolted
provinces, they have aimed at making conqueſts;
—They have compleated their guilt by a daring
attempt to annex your immenfe province of Canada, to the empire they have newly ſet up.—And
now, what can I ſay in their behalf?—My grand
plea,

---

* I would not dare to uſe fuch an expreſſion, if the ſcripture
did not bear me out. The Lord, ſpeaking by the prophet Mala-
chi, ſays, *Will a man* ROB GOD? *Yet ye have* ROBBED ME. *But
ye ſay, Wherein have we* ROBBED THEE?—*In* TITHES. Mal.
iii. 8.—I infer from this anſwer, that if GOD accounts himſelf
robbed, when *tithes* are detained from HIS *prieſts*; he does ſo
much more, when reaſonable and legal *taxes* are detained from
ſovereigns, HIS primary repreſentatives, whom he calls HIS
anointed, and to whom he allows the title of *gods.*

plea, O ye infulted powers, is taken from your
felves. *As your majefty is, fo is your mercy.*—Ye ar^e
called *chriftians* by the name of the mild Potentate'
who are interceded for his mobbing murderers. When
they poured floods of contempt upon his royal head ;
—when they pierced his temples with thorns, his
hands with nails, his heart with farcafms ;—and
when they prepared to pierce his fide with a fpear ;
even *then*, he not only forgave them himfelf, but
turned their excufer and faid, *Father, forgive them,*
for *they know not what they do.* The divine plea prevailed. It obtained an evangelical proclamation of
pardon on the moft condefcending terms. *Where fin
had abounded, there grace did much more abound.*
Where rebellion had fet up her bloody banner, there
mercy gloried to erect her fuperior ftandard. Jerufalem, ungrateful, hypocritical, rebellious Jerufalem ;—Jerufalem, guilty of the murder of the King
of kings :—Jerufalem, the ftill rebellious and unre-
lenting city, was *firft* bleffed with the news of a free
pardon ; and thoufands of relenting rebels fubmitted
to the terms of the gracious proclamation. By this
unexpected effort of mercy, the Lord of glory fub-
jugated thofe ftiff religionifts. Pardoning love effectually conquered their ftubbornefs ; and *a nation of
loyal fubjects was not born in a day.*
And might ye not, O ye chriftian Rulers, imitate *the Lord of glory* without proftituting your dignity ?—Directed by the example of our meek Re-
deemer, might not thy mercy, O king, iffue out a
proclamation of pardon, upon fuch terms as might
raife the aftonifhment of an *Adams* and a *Wafhing-
ton?* Are *Lee* and *Hancock* fiercer againft thee,
than *Saul* of Tarfus was againft his Saviour ? Have
they breathed out more threatenings and flaughter
than that enthufiaftic zealot, who, not fatisfied with
his perfonal contempt of the Lord of lords, compelled others to blafpheme him, and perfecuted to
death thofe who would not ? Neverthelefs, when
he fell to the ground, mercy raifed him up, not
only to the dignity of a chriftian, but to that of an

Apostle : And the service which he did the church in that high office, far exceeded the injury he had done her by his bloody enthusiasm. Could ye not, O ye christian Legislators, try the same successful method with your American subjects ? If *Mercy alone* would make them insolent; and if *Power alone* would make them desperate ; could not power and mercy combined by your wisdom, effectually disarm them, and for ever attach them to your steady and mild government ?

Nor will you by this means overcome the Americans alone. You will also disarm the minority of your respectable body, and their numerous partisans in the kingdom. When we are wrongfully accused of intending things we never thought of, does not prudence call upon us to remove the very appearances, by which the charge *seems* supported ? And how can these *appearances* be *fully* removed in the present case, otherwise than by granting your American subjects the privilege of *some direct representation*, together with *some security*, that the taxes laid upon them shall always bear an equitable proportion to the taxes laid upon your British subjects ?

Might I not also presume to ask, if all the grievances they complain of are imaginary, and if no *needless provocation* has been given them by some of our countrymen, and no *secret encouragement* by others ? Besides, are ye not divided among yourselves ? And if ye have taught them the unhappy art of rising against you, by rising against each other, should ye not pity them ? And should ye not bear *a little* with their turbulency, since you are obliged to bear *so much* from those of your own body, who openly countenance their rash patriotism ?

Again : If ye are the political *Parents* of the Colonists, are they not entitled to parental indulgence from you ? *My Lord the King is as an angel of God, to discern good and bad :* He knows, and ye, his legislative assessors, know, that *political*, as well as religious *enthusiasm* is a fever of the mind.

mind, which throws thofe, who are attacked with it, into a temporary delirium; and that, in the paroxyfm, heated religionifts and patriots, like delirious people, fay and do a thoufand things, of which they are afhamed when they come to themfelves again. If your own children were dangeroufly ill and light-headed, would ye not treat them with an indulgence fuitable to their deplorable cafe? And would not natural affection concur with reafon, to make you overlook the petulance and wildnefs of their behaviour? Ye will extend your mercy to your American fubjects with double readinefs, if ye confider, that they are not all guilty. A few warm men among them opened the flood-gates of patriotic licentioufnefs: and whilft the fierce and roaring torrent *frightened* myriads into a *temporary* compliance to revolt; it carried away myriads more, before they knew what they were about. Nor have they perhaps had it yet in their power to recollect themfelves. Vouchfafe then to fhew yourfelves their *tender phyficians*, as well as their *indulgent parents*; nor heal their moral fever by burning corrofives, fo long as there is the leaft profpect of doing it by cooling applications. If chriftianity commands us to *reftore in the fpirit of meeknefs thofe that are fallen*, to *become weak to the weak*, yea, to *become all things to all men, that by all means* we *may gain and fave fome*; be abundantly condefcending to your American people, that you may *fave* thoufands of precious lives, prevent the devaftation of your own dominions, and difappoint your enemies, who flatter themfelves, that, when Great Britain and her Colonies fhall have exhaufted their ftrength in a deftructive war, the Britifh empire, or fome part of it, will become an eafy prey to their greedy and watchful ambition.

But I peculiarly addrefs thee, Thou majeftic *Head*, and executive *Hand* of the legiflative power. By thy fteadinefs thou haft fhewn thyfelf a King worthy of commanding a people, who difplay lions in their ftandards. And now like *Meffiah*, the

Prince, like the generous *Lion of the tribe of Judah*, vouchfafe to fhew thyfelf *the Prince of peace*. Let all the earth know, that thou art a reprefentative of the GOD *of all grace*, and of *the* LAMB *that taketh away the fin of the world*. Is not the right of fhewing mercy to the condemned, the nobleft of all 'thy royal prerogatives, and the brighteft jewel of thy imperial crown? Oh! let that jewel fhine in this cloudy day, and it will reflect the light of the *fun of righteoufnefs* acrofs the Atlantic, and chear the weftern world. The proclamation of a general pardon, accompanied by the grant of a direct reprefentation, and of a fecurity for the equitable proportion, which their taxes fhall always bear to ours;—fuch a proclamation, I fay, enforced by the found of thy trumpets, the roar of thy cannons, the fight of thy fleets, and the terror of thy armies, will fhew, that thou art eminently qualified to reign over a brave and free people. Thou mayeft thus be merciful without weaknefs. A *Lee* and a *Washington* are refolute enough to ftand for a time the fhock of thy forces: An *Adams* and an *Hancock* are obftinate enough to bury themfelves in the ruins of their country :. But, refolute and obftinate as they are, thy mercy confounds— thine indulgence difarms them.—The paroxifm is over.—Candor and loyalty return together.—Thy fiery heroes come back to fober heroifm; and the rafh patriots, to true patriotifm.—Thy royal mercy has melted them into tears.—With fhame they fix their weeping eyes to the ground; with admiration they lift them up to heaven.—They claim the honour of bringing in perfon the reftitution-money, thou infifteft upon for thy injured fubjects. —They hafte to throw themfelves at the feet of a Sovereign, who knows how to protect, conquer, and pardon.—My imagination fees them crofs the Atlantic:—They enter your gates:—They throw American 'fwords at your feet:—They afk pardon for themfelves, and the guilty people they reprefent:—They kifs the royal hand, which has averted

their

their impending ruin, and pour out their grateful
fouls in fuch words as thefe.

" MERCIFUL and Great King, and Ye, his legiflative affeffors, permit us to diftinguifh ourfelves
by our penitential return, as we once did by our
rafh revolt. With feelings proportionable to the
fenfe we have of our guilt, of the king's mercy,
and the parliament's condefcention, we lament our
mifapprehenfions; and deploring the bloodfhed
which they have caufed, we acknowledge that we
owe you the reafonable taxes due to the fupreme,
protecting power, by the confent of all civilized
nations, and by the exprefs command of God; and
fince you condefcend to grant us the privilege of a
fhare in your legiflature, we will not only religioufly, but *chearfully*, pay them for the time to
come. In the mean while, we refund at your feet
fums equivalent to the goods, which our rafh citizens buried in the fea; and we own it is juft, that
we fhould, in due proportion, help to difch rge the
national debt, which has been in part contracted
for our protection, and which our unhappy revolt
has of late fo greatly increafed. Made wifer by
our misfortunes, and taught both to revere and love
our mother-country, we fhall, at every proper opportunity, exprefs our grateful fenfe of her parental
regard. We are indeed feparated by the Atlantic
ocean, which we lately looked upon as a bounda-
ry to your dominions, a vaft moat to keep us afun-
der, and a watery rampart to defend our continent
againft your incurfions: But now our views are
changed, and we confider that wide fea as a mag-
nificent channel, which divine providence feems
to have prepared, to facilitate our friendly and
commercial intercourfe;—to enrich our refpective
countries with the treafures of the old and new
world;—to make us live in a conftant exercife of
the art of navigation,—and enable us, by this
means, powerfully to fupport the Britifh claims to
the empire of the fea.—Such are the pleafing
thoughts we have of our happy re-union. May

they

they appear equally delightful to all, who wiſh well
to the Britiſh empire! And may the poiſonous
breath of diſcord, more dangerous than all the
ſtorms of the Atlantic, never break the ſweet calm,
which royal mercy and parliamentary condeſcen-
ſion have reſtored to our diſtracted provinces !"

" Take up your ſwords, ye brave, though
raſh, patriots, replies the Speaker. Your courage
and love of liberty entitle you to the honour of receiving them again, on condition that you beat
them into plowſhares, or uſe them only againſt our
common enemies. It is the *firſt*—ſee that it be the
laſt time, they are ſtained with Britiſh blood, and
lifted up againſt the breaſt, that gave you ſuck.
And as the world ſees the political and military
leaders of the Colonies at the foot of the Throne,
and of a Britiſh ſenate ; the world ſhall ſee, that the
king and parliament can not only

Parcere ſubjectis, et debellare ſuperbos,

but that they know how to conquer the generous
friends of liberty, by generous acts of conde-
ſcending love. Riſe, ye miſtaken ſons of liberty,—riſe to demonſtrate, that, as we can *fight* like
Britains, ſo we can *forgive* as chriſtians, and *in-
dulge* as brethren. Take your ſeats among Britiſh
ſenators, and particularly repreſent the American
Provinces. But beware of conſidering this privilege as a *bribe* beſtowed by a timorous adminiſtration,—much leſs as a *reward* for your raſh revolt.
Though we make allowances for your miſtakes,
and put a favourable conſtruction upon your inten-
tions, we abhor and bear our ſolemn teſtimony
againſt your proceedings. But the mantle of royal
mercy, and of your repentance having covered all,
we ſhall not upbraid you with antichriſtian principles, and bloody ſcenes, which we wiſh buried in
eternal oblivion. If we grant you ſome ſeats in
the

the houfe of Commons, it is only to remove your
jealoufies by a condefcenfion, which becomes a mother-country and a mild government ; and to regain
the filial confidence of our American Colonies by per-
mitting the men, who have been moft prejudiced
againft us, to be eye witneffes of our firm attach-
ment to the conftitution, of our impartial zeal for the
dignity of the crown, of our guardian care for the
conftitutional liberty of the people, and of our prudent endeavours to fecure the due obedience of the
Britifh fubjects."

 " The wound which the demon of Difcord has
given to our union, cannot be perfectly healed but
by an *amputation* or a *confolidation*. The former
expedient is inconfiftent with our mutual affection,
and our common intereft : But the latter is perfectly
agreeable to both. And our confanguinity loudly
demands that it fhould be preferred. Help us then
to confolidate the lacerated parts of the Britifh empire. Let our filial gratitude meet our paternal condefcenfion half way : So fhall reconciling love caft
the bridge of union acrofs the Atlantic, and firmly
join our happy ifland with your fortunate continent :
And may genuine, fober, fcriptural patriotifin, like
an adamantine key, for ever bind the folid arch !
May one blood—one language—one conftitution—
one religion—one king—one fupreme legiflature—
one temporal and eternal intereft, combine to make
us one flourifhing empire, till the kingdom of God
fwallow up all other kingdoms ! Nor let it be faid
any more,

    Audiet cives acuiffe ferrum,
    Quo graves *Turcæ* melius perirent;
    Audiet pugnas, vitio parentum
        Rara juventus."†

                                        Whilft

---

† Our pofterity thinned by our civil wars, will hear of our
culpable contentions, and will lament our having turned againft
each other thofe fwords, which fhould never have been drawn
but againft our common enemies.

Whilft the Speaker concludes this patriotic fpeech, my imagination returns from her pleafing excur-fion. The awful, parliamentary fcene vanifhes " like the bafelefs fabric of a vifion." But " a wreck is left behind :" Hints of a *fcriptural* method of reconciliation are humbly fuggefted; and you have fome expreffions of my cordial concern for the glory of our Sovereign, and the fatisfaction of our American fellow-fubjects, to whom, as well as to Dr. Price and yourfelf, I fincerely wifh all the fweets of Chriftian and Britifh liberty, without any of the bitters of religious and civil licentioufnefs. *Of mak-ing many books*, fays Solomon, *there is no end. Let us* then *hear the conclufion of the whole matter : Fear God and keep his Commandments, for this is the whole duty of man.*—Or, if you prefer St. Peter's words, *Fear God and honour the King,* for this is the fum of the two tables of *Chrifi's law.* That, inftead of break-ing one of thefe tables under pretence of keeping the other, we may always agree to pay a chearful obedience to both, is the final and higheft wifh of

> *Rev. Sir,*
>
> Your obedient fervant in a gofpel, which *neither makes void the law thro' faith,* nor fuperfedes loyalty thro' liberty.
>
> J. F.

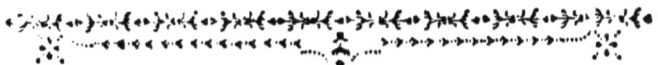

POSTSCRIPT.

I HAVE obferved, p. 84, that the fpecies of patriotifm which I oppofe, is a vicious temper " compounded of one or more of the following in-gredients; prejudice, ignorance, conceit, pride, ambi-

ambition, refractorinefs, &c." As you may think
Sir, that this defcription is too fevere, I beg leave to
fupport it by the account that an honeft inhabitant
of *Pennfylvania* [who is eye-witnefs to the workings
of American patriotifm] gives his friend in England,
of what you call American *liberty*, and what I beg
leave to call American *tyrranny*. As I can depend
on his veracity, I prefent you with the following
extract from his original letter, which is now before
me.

" March 12, 1776.—Letters are not fmuggled
hence with little difficulty and rifque, as every
thing we write may be infpected by the jaundiced
eye of men, who jefuitically conftrue the moft
guarded words of *Englifhmen* inimical to *America* ;
deterring examples of which are not wanting.—
With pretence of obtaining privileges, the inhabi-
tants of this country lofe the enjoyment of their privileges. Under mafk of liberty, and cry of grievances, a fet of ambitious men and defigning demagogues *wrigled*" [got] " themfelves in power,
which they unwarrantably exercifed in abolifhing
law, juftice, the freedom of the prefs, fpeech, and
action ;—in feizing all the channels of intelligence;
—in publifhing and inculcating the moft fhocking,
wicked, and malicious falfhoods.—By fpecious pre-
texts, artful diffimulation, and obftinate efforts,
thefe enemies to truth, affronters of juftice, and vio-
laters of laws, have not only poifoned and inflamed
the minds of the people ; but have influenced them
fo far as to take and pafs current 4 by 3 inches of
printed brown paper for no lefs than fix guineas ;
by all thefe means leading the duped inftruments of
their ambition, with monftrous ftrides, towards their
own and country's ruin."

" Had I a hundred mouths, a hundred tongues,
   A voice of brafs, and adamantine lungs;
   Not half the mighty fcene could I difclofe,
   Repeat their crimes, or count our matchlefs
     woes."

" I affer

" I affert thefe naked and glaring truths, with a confidence which cannot be fhaken, &c."

Our letter-writer after obferving, that the compliance of the majority " to fuch tyranny" is but " paffive;" and that the proportion of thofe, who take an active part in it, is " about one in ten of the whole community," adds what follows: " To fee men of reputed fenfe, fome by their paffive, and others by their active conduct, manifefting fuch ignorance and blindnefs to the true intereft of themfelves, their country, and pofterity, makes me think at times,

> " Perhaps he whofe hand the lightning forms,
>   Who heaves old Ocean, and who wings the
>   ftorms,
>   Pours fierce ambition into *Hancock*'s mind;
>   Or turns young *Adams* loofe, to fcourge man-
>   kind,"

" and permit irreligious Britons to plunge themfelves into difficulties, both to chaftife them for, and turn them from, the evil of their doings."

The letter-writer, after wifhing that " the councils on both fides may be bleffed with that wifdom and moderation, which may be productive of a permanent union, fo neceffary to the welfare of both countries," adds in a poftfcript: " I enclofe this in a bottle of Cream of Tartar directed to a paffenger on board, in hope that having occafion to ufe it, this might be found, and thereby efcape."

Had I feen this American account of American patriotifm, before I fent my laft letter to the printer; I would have pleaded lefs earneftly for *fome* of the patriots than I have done. But I do not ftop the prefs, becaufe condefcenfion is the fafer extreme; and becaufe experience teaches England, that American patriots do their country lefs mifchief in the manfion-houfe, and in the parliament, than in the tower and in a common jail.

Permit

Permit me, Sir, to conclude by a remark upon
the character, which the Monthly Reviewers give
me in their laft Review.   They call me " a mere
" *Sacheverel* : a preacher of thofe flavifh and jufily
" exploded jacobitical doctrines, for which the me-
" mory of *Sacheverel* and his abettors will ever be
" held in equal contempt and abhorrence by every
" true friend of the liberties of mankind ?" I
fhould be truly forry if I deferved fo fevere a cen-
fure : I hope that the Reviewers have paffed it with
a degree of precipitation.   Poffibly they did not
read fo far in my *Vindication* as page 63, &c. or
even p. 40, where I begin to guard my doctrine
againft the *Jacobitical* tenets of defpotifm. Should
my *American Patriotifm* reach thofe gentlemen, and
fhould they give themfelves the trouble to turn to
pages 8, 14, 17, 37, 38, 59, 61, 63, 65, where
I continue to guard Britifh liberty againft the encroachments of arbitrary power, I flatter myfelf
that they will fee, I am no more " *a mere Sacheverel*" than I am *a mere Price*. Dr. *Sacheverel* ran
as fiercely into the *high monarchial* extreme, as Dr.
Price does into the *high republican* extreme. I have
endeavoured to keep at an equal diftance from their
oppofite miftakes, by contending only for the juft
medium, which the holy fcriptures and our excellent conftitution point out; and I hope my *unprejudiced* readers will do me the juftice to confefs,
that, if I have miffed the mark of moderation, at
which I fincerely aim, I have not miffed it [*toto cœlo*]
by going full eaft with Dr. *Sacheverel*, any more
than by going full weft with Dr. *Price*. What has
poffibly mifled the Reviewers, is their not confidering, that my withftanding an opponent, who im-
petuoufly throws himfelf into the levelling extreme
of Dr. *Price*, obliges me *principally* to oppofe *this*
extreme. If Dr. *Sacheverel* were alive, and his
erroneous, enthufiaftical, mobbing politicks en-
dangered the public tranquility, as the patriotifm
                                                    of

of Mr. *Evans* and Dr. *Price* does at prefent; I would oppofe the *high churchman*, as much as I nc do the two *high diffenters*. Before we abfolute condemn an author, we fhould, I think, confid what extreme *times* and *circumftances* call him chie to guard againft. But party-men feldom do this and it is well if, after all, bigotted *anti-Americe* do not blame fome parts of this publication, : much as *Americanus* will blame other parts. *Moc* ration has not many friends whilft the fpirit of co tention runs high; but, like *wifdom*, fhe *is juftifi of her children*, and will in time win fome of h oppofers.

When the Reviewers have given me the charact of a " *mere Sacheverel*," we may naturally expec to fee them recommend your performance as muc as they decry mine: accordingly they fay, " M " Evans is a lively and fenfible advocate for tl " freedom of the Colonies, a fpirited controvertif " &c.—In letter iii. Mr. F's reafons from *fcriptu* " are fhewn to be inconfiftent, abfurd, and total. " inconclufive."—To fhew how ftrongly the judg ment of ingenious critics may be biaffed by prejudic I need only refer our readers to p. 12, &c. where produce the " lively and fenfible" arguments, b which you attempt to prove, that my fcripture do trine of taxation is " abfurd."

THE END.

www.ingramcontent.com/pod-product-compliance
Lightning Source LLC
Chambersburg PA
CBHW031439280326
41927CB00038B/1060